PAPER WARPLANES

David Hawcock

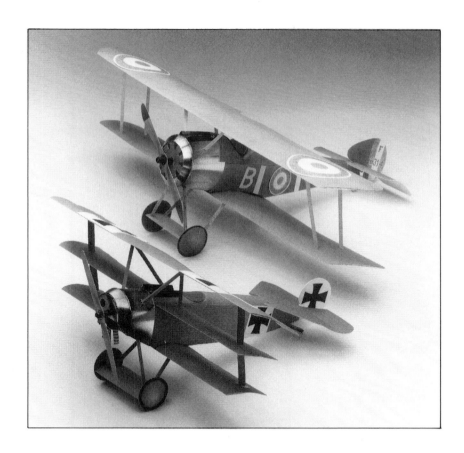

DAVID & CHARLES
Newton Abbot   London

British Library Cataloguing in Publication Data

Hawcock, David
    Paper warplanes.
    1. Paper aeroplanes. Making — Manuals — For children
    I. Title
    745.592

    ISBN 0-7153-9366-9

Typeset by Typesetters (Birmingham) Ltd,
Smethwick, West Midlands
and printed in Great Britain
by Redwood Burn, Trowbridge, Wiltshire
for David & Charles Publishers plc
Brunel House   Newton Abbot   Devon

CONTENTS

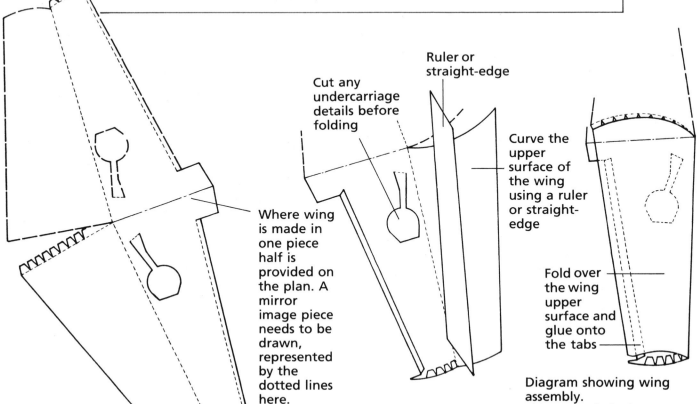

Where wing is made in one piece half is provided on the plan. A mirror image piece needs to be drawn, represented by the dotted lines here.

Cut any undercarriage details before folding

Ruler or straight-edge

Curve the upper surface of the wing using a ruler or straight-edge

Fold over the wing upper surface and glue onto the tabs

Diagram showing wing assembly.
This example is the Messerschmitt 109 but the principle is the same for all of the planes in the book.

INTRODUCTION

The twelve aeroplanes in this book span almost the entire history of military aviation. It is quite astonishing to consider just how rapidly advances have been made from the canvas and wood biplanes of World War I to modern computerised aircraft. All these changes have occurred virtually within living memory. Sir Thomas Sopwith, who died in 1989 aged 101, was easily the most innovative aircraft designer on the Allied side during World War I; he was also responsible for the Hawker Hurricane in World War II and was involved in the development of the Harrier Jump Jet whose vertical take off abilities are considered to be the most revolutionary war plane advance since the jet engine. As you assemble the models contained in this book, just consider that if so much has been achieved in so little time what spectacular air, and perhaps space, craft the future may bring.

The World War I aircraft are probably the most demanding of the models, so try one of the others first, such as the Messerschmitt or the F-111, just to get your hand in.

The first step in making each model is to enlarge the plans to the desired size. This can be done by hand, but a simpler method is to use an enlarging photocopier – there should be one available at your local photocopy shop or office stationers. As all the models employ the same method of wing assembly this is explained by line diagrams on the contents page, rather than repeating the same instructions twelve times.

All the models illustrated have been assembled from cartridge paper torn from a sketch pad. It is easiest to decorate the models before assembly. Paint, felt tipped pens and coloured pencils are all suitable for this task. The silver models are also cut from cartridge paper which has been covered with cooking foil, but it is possible to find silver paper of the correct thickness if preferred. The engine cowling on the Fokker and Camel are made from silver card.

With the exception of the helicopter, all the aircraft can be made to glide. The models which make the best gliders are the Camel, the Fokker, the F-111 and the Harrier. Due to their weight and bulkiness, the Lancaster and Lightning make less successful gliders. All you need to do to enable your model to take to the air is strengthen any weak areas, for example the wing struts and undercarriage on the Sopwith Camel and Fokker Dr 1. Do this by using sheets of thicker paper glued together or match sticks. To prevent the model 'stalling' in flight simply counterweight the nose with a *small* piece of plasticine or several paperclips. Start with a very light weight and build up to the correct amount by carrying out test flights.

Enjoy yourself!

Sopwith Camel

The Sopwith Camel was Britain's most successful World War I fighter, first seeing action in June 1917. The Camel was not the first allied aircraft to be fitted with machine-gun synchronisation gear (which enabled a gun to fire through the propeller without damaging it), but it was the first fitted with *two* synchronised guns, which significantly increased firepower . . . and the 'hump' covering the guns led to the aircraft's name.

During the war, 5,490 Camels were built. They were powered by a variety of rotary engines – 110hp Le Rhone, 110hp or 130hp Clerget or 150hp BR1 Bentley. A top speed of around 115mph and a high degree of manoeuvrability coupled with a ceiling of 19,600ft made the Camel a match for any German aircraft.

Camels scored a total of 1,294 victories. The most famous pilot to fly the Camel was the Canadian Captain Roy Brown of No 209 Squadron, Royal Air Force. On 21 April 1918, Brown shot down 'The Red Baron', the Camel's most famous victim.

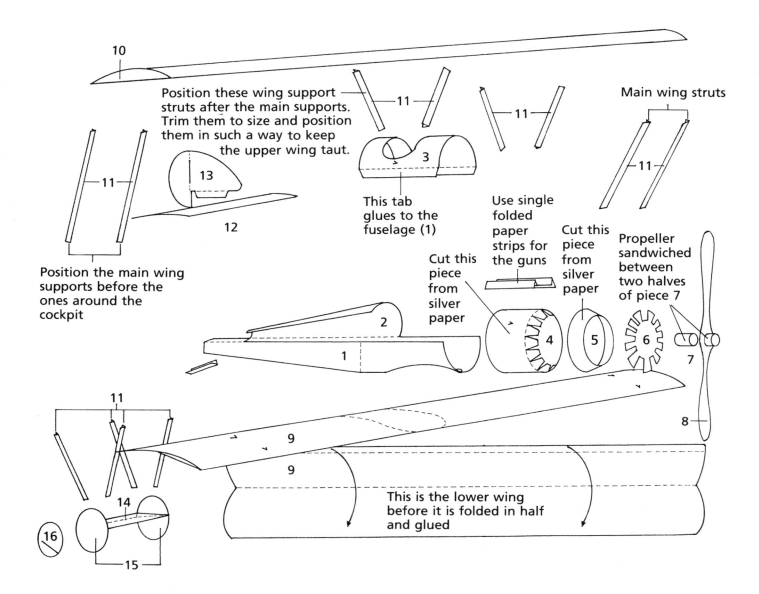

Position these wing support struts after the main supports. Trim them to size and position them in such a way to keep the upper wing taut.

10

11

11

Main wing struts

11

13

3

11

This tab glues to the fuselage (1)

12

11

Position the main wing supports before the ones around the cockpit

Use single folded paper strips for the guns

Cut this piece from silver paper

Cut this piece from silver paper

Propeller sandwiched between two halves of piece 7

Cut this piece from silver paper

2

1

4

5

6

7

8

11

9

9

This is the lower wing before it is folded in half and glued

14

16

15

Sopwith Camel

1 Fold piece 1 into shape. Curve piece 2 and glue into position. Curve the cockpit (3) and glue this in place.
2 Cut piece 4 from silver paper, fold it into a cylinder and join it to the body. Cut 5 from silver paper, fold it into a ring and glue it to piece 4. Insert and glue in place the engine (6). Make a short, tight roll of paper (7), cut it in half and sandwich the propeller between the two parts. Glue to the centre of the engine.
3 Assemble the lower wing (9). Glue it in place on the body. Assemble the upper wing (10).
4 To join the upper and lower wings cut out piece 11 four times and fold each piece in half. Cut tiny 'V' slits in the

lower wing and slot and glue each strut in place. When these have dried lower the upper wing into position and glue. Cut another four of piece 11, and use to secure the wing to the cockpit (3) and engine cowling (4), trimming the pieces to size to achieve a rigid wing position.
5 Fold and assemble the tailplane (12). Glue into position at the end of the fuselage. Glue piece 13 in place.
6 To make the undercarriage fold piece 14 into a wedge shape. Using four more struts (11) secure this to the cowling (4) and lower wing (9).
7 Glue the wheels (15) in place. Form a cone from each piece 16 and glue onto the wheels to represent hubs.

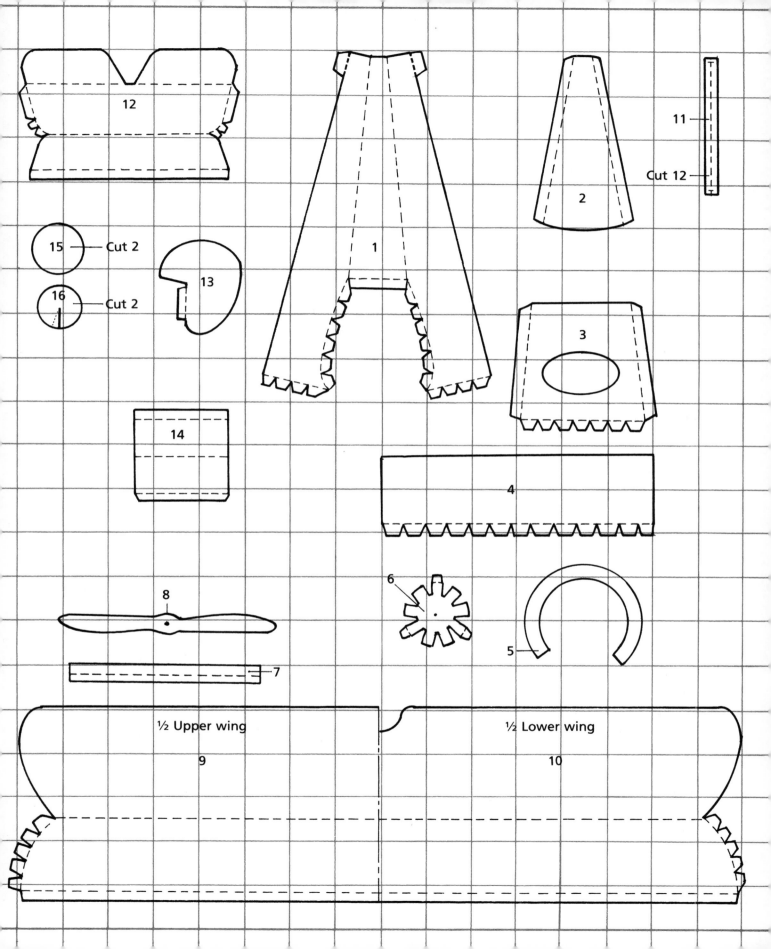

Fokker Dr 1

The Fokker *Dreidekker*, designed by Anthony Fokker specifically as a 'dog fighter', had a wing span of only 23ft 7½ inches. Powered by a 110hp Oberursel URII or Thulin-built Le Rhone 9J rotary, the Dr 1 had a maximum speed of 103mph, a ceiling of 19,600ft and an astonishing rate of climb for the period – 2,000ft per minute.

Manfred von Richthofen 'The Red Baron' was the most renowned Dr 1 pilot, scoring eighty victories before being shot down. Another Dr 1 ace, Werner Voss, encountered seven Allied SE 5A fighters whilst flying alone and shot holes in all seven aircraft before falling to 2nd Lt. A. P .F. Rhys-Davids.

9

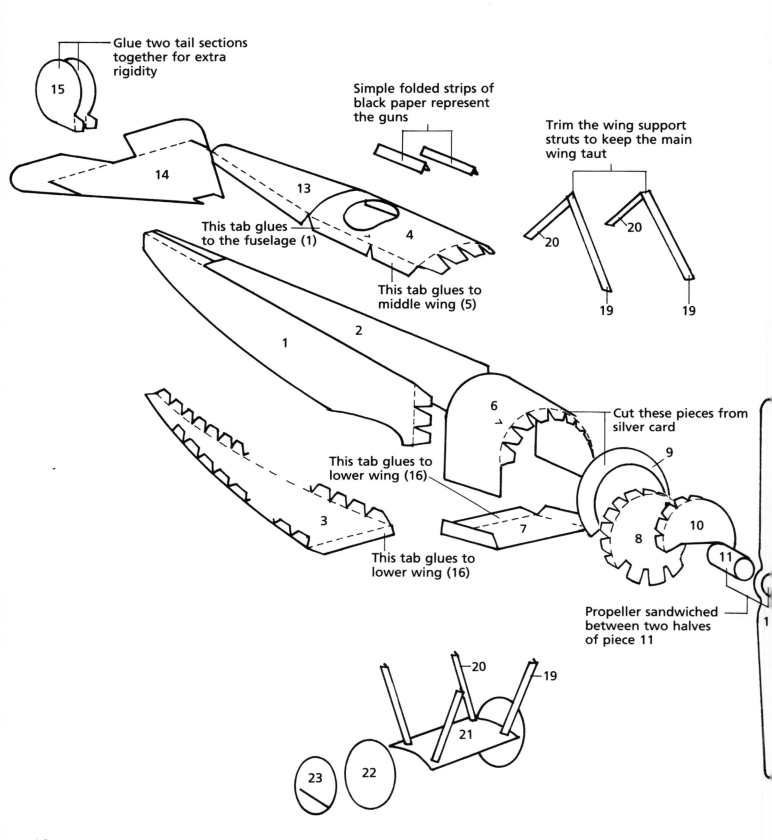

Glue two tail sections together for extra rigidity

15

Simple folded strips of black paper represent the guns

Trim the wing support struts to keep the main wing taut

14

13

4

This tab glues to the fuselage (1)

This tab glues to middle wing (5)

20

20

20

19

19

2

1

6

Cut these pieces from silver card

9

This tab glues to lower wing (16)

7

10

3

8

11

This tab glues to lower wing (16)

Propeller sandwiched between two halves of piece 11

1

20

19

21

23

22

Fokker
Dr 1

1 Assemble the fuselage from pieces 1, 2, and 3.
2 Gently curve the cockpit (4) and glue into the fuselage using the back two tabs only.
3 Fold up the middle wing (5) and slip this between the cockpit (4) and pieces 1 and 2. Secure in place using remaining tabs.
4 Cut out and curve the engine cowling (6). Glue it in place and make secure by positioning piece 7. Insert the engine (8) just behind the tabs on piece 6. Curve piece 9 and attach it to piece 6. Insert 10 into the engine.
5 Make a tight roll of paper (11), cut it in half, sandwich the propeller (12) between the two parts and glue into place.
6 Curve piece 13 into shape and position it behind the cockpit.
7 Glue the tailplane (14) into place. Cut two of piece 15, stick together and glue between fuselage pieces 1 and 2

8 Assemble the lower wing (16) and secure in place on the underside of the fuselage between pieces 7 and 3.
9 Cut out two wing struts (17). Make tiny 'V' slits in the middle wing (5) and slide the struts through, glueing them onto the lower wing (16). Ensure that the wings remain parallel. Fold up the main wing (18) and position on to the top of the wing struts. Secure the main wing by positioning pieces 19 and 20. Secure the upper wing (18) to the fuselage (4) and engine cowling (6) trimming to size to achieve a rigid wing position.
10 Assemble the undercarriage. Fold up piece 21, attach struts 19 and 20. Glue the assembly onto piece 7 and wing 16.
11 Complete the model by sticking wheels (22) in place on piece 21. Fold piece 23 into a shallow cone and stick one on each wheel to represent hubs.

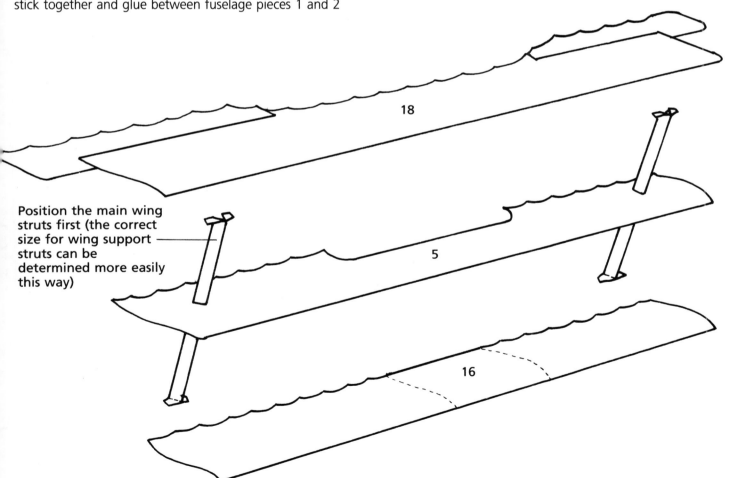

Position the main wing struts first (the correct size for wing support struts can be determined more easily this way)

18

5

16

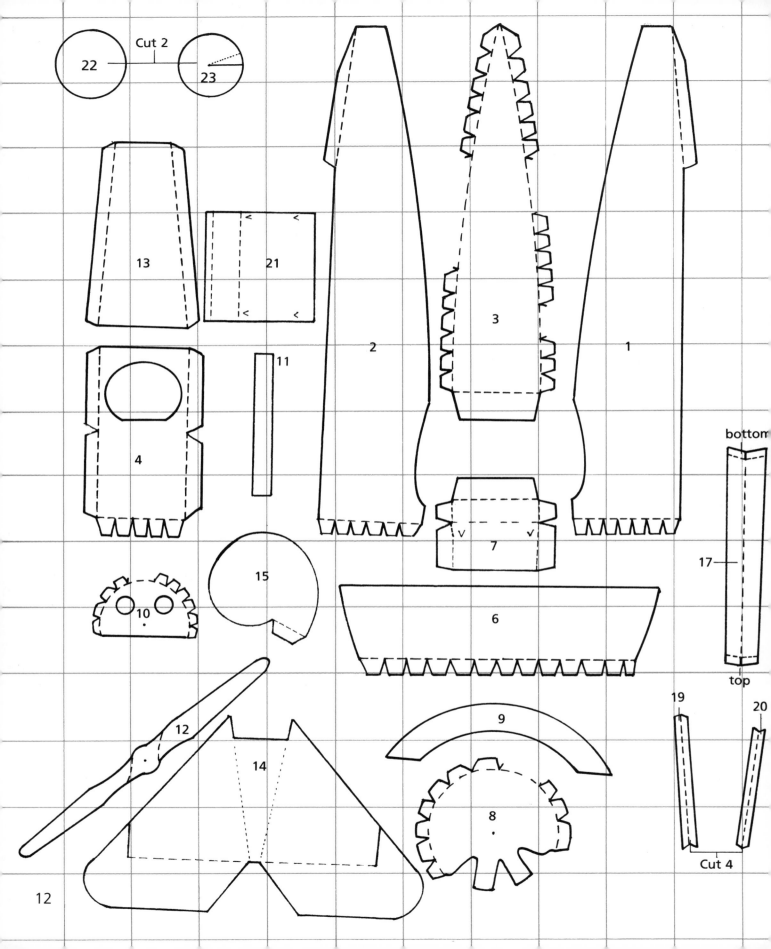

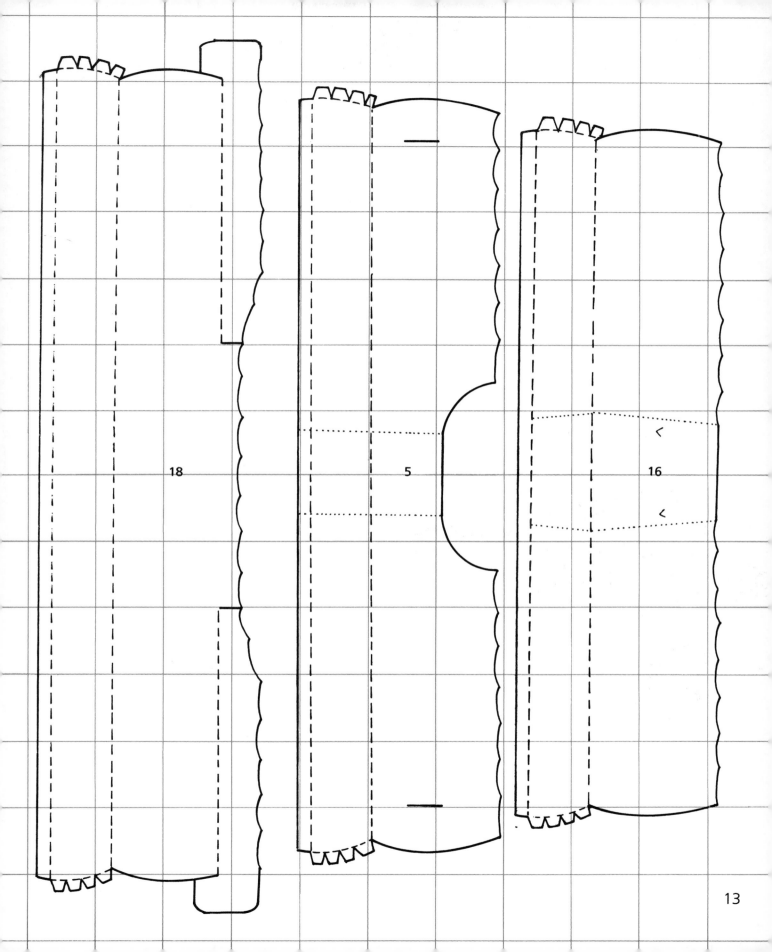

18

5

16

13

Messerschmitt Bf 109

The Messerschmitt Bf 109 was the most numerous German fighter of World War II, serving throughout the conflict in a series of improved models. Powerful and highly manoeuvrable, it was considered to be at least the equal of the Spitfire. However, during the critical phases of the Battle of Britain in 1940, its qualities were restrained by the tactics employed by the *Luftwaffe*. The Bf 109E-1 of the Battle of Britain had a top speed of 354mph and a service ceiling of 36,000 feet. In comparison, the Bf 109K-4 of the last year of the war, 1945, had a top speed of 452mph and a service ceiling of 41,000 feet.

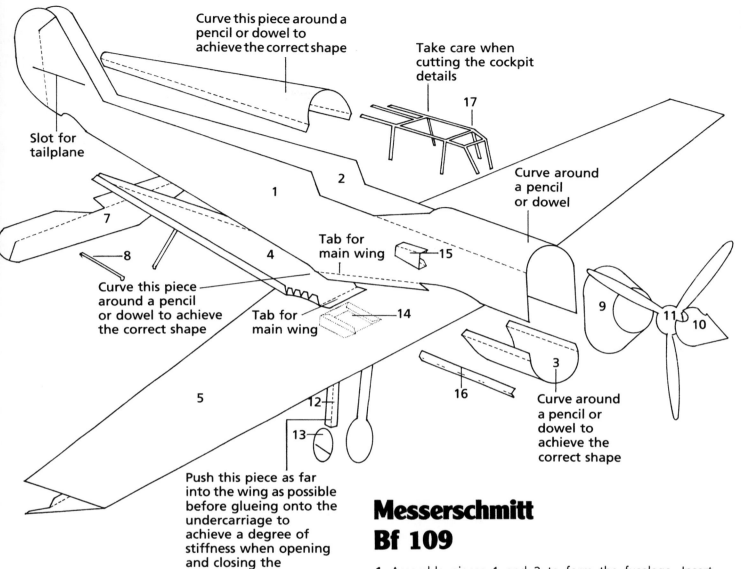

Curve this piece around a pencil or dowel to achieve the correct shape

Take care when cutting the cockpit details

17

Slot for tailplane

2

1

7

Curve around a pencil or dowel

8

Tab for main wing

15

Curve this piece around a pencil or dowel to achieve the correct shape

4

Tab for main wing

14

9

11

10

5

16

3

12

13

Curve around a pencil or dowel to achieve the correct shape

Push this piece as far into the wing as possible before glueing onto the undercarriage to achieve a degree of stiffness when opening and closing the undercarriage.

Messerschmitt Bf 109

1 Assemble pieces 1 and 2 to form the fuselage. Insert pieces 3 and 4.

2 Assemble the main wing (5) and glue onto the fuselage.

3 Make up the tailplane by glueing piece 6 under 7. Slot the completed tail into the fuselage. Support it with two small struts (8).

4 Curve the nose cone (9) into a ring and attach it to the fuselage. Make up the spinner (10), slot in the propeller (11) and glue it to the nose cone.

5 To strengthen the undercarriage cut and fold two of piece 12 and glue in place. Make each piece 13 into a cone and attach to the wheel to represent hubs.

6 Cut out two radiators (14) and glue them on the underside of the main wing to each side of the centre. Attach piece 15 to the side of the engine along with the exhausts (16).

7 Fold and attach the cockpit window (17).

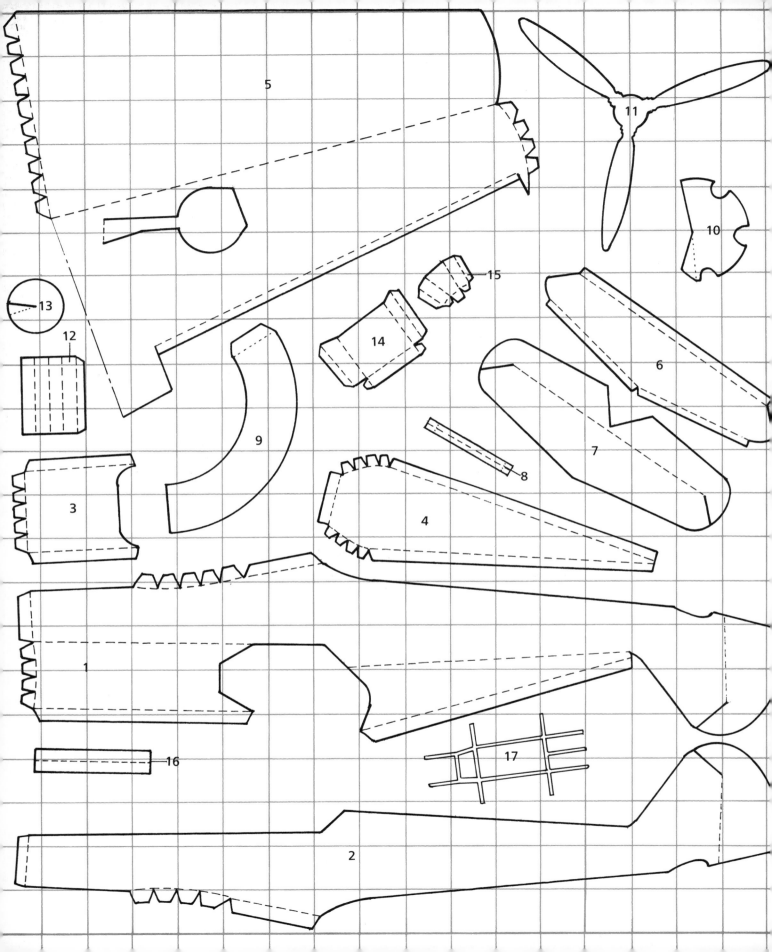

Spitfire

Designed by Reginald L. Mitchell, the Spitfire is the most memorable aircraft from World War II. Its characteristic elliptical wing has become a symbol of the Battle of Britain. Like the Hurricane, the Spitfire was created for one purpose: to defend Britain against the German *Luftwaffe.*

The Spitfire F Mk VB was powered by a 1,470hp Rolls-Royce Merlin 45 engine giving it a top speed of 369mph, and a service ceiling of 36,200ft. The aircraft had a 36ft 10 inch wing span.

As the Spitfire's performance was not notably greater than that of its main adversaries, much of the aircraft's success must be attributed to 'The Few' who flew them. By the end of World War II, no fewer than 20,351 Spitfires had been produced.

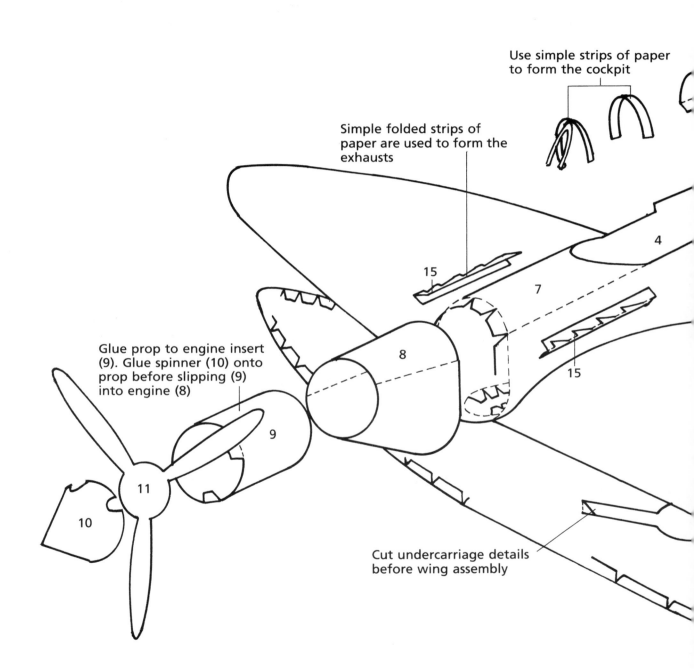

Use simple strips of paper
to form the cockpit

Simple folded strips of
paper are used to form the
exhausts

15

4

7

15

8

Glue prop to engine insert
(9). Glue spinner (10) onto
prop before slipping (9)
into engine (8)

9

11

10

Cut undercarriage details
before wing assembly

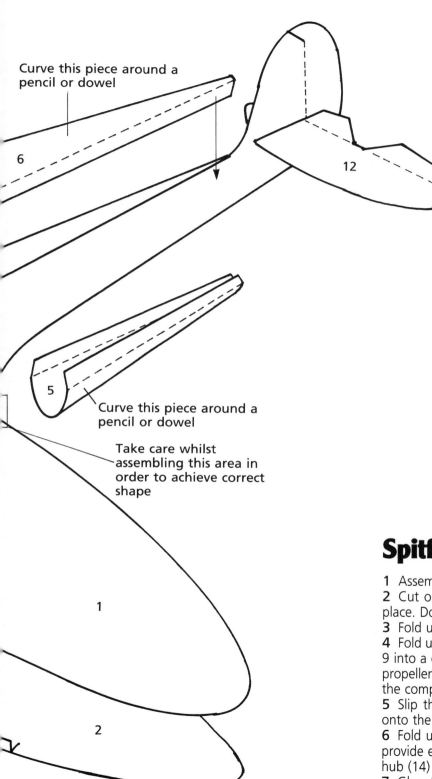

Curve this piece around a pencil or dowel

6

Curve this piece around a pencil or dowel

5

Take care whilst assembling this area in order to achieve correct shape

12

1

2

Spitfire

1 Assemble the main wing, gently curving piece 1.

2 Cut out pieces 3 and 4. Curve piece 5, then glue it in place. Do the same with piece 6.

3 Fold up piece 7 and glue in place.

4 Fold up the nose cone (8) and glue in place. Curve piece 9 into a cylinder. Make a cone from piece 10. Position the propeller to fit into the spinner (10) and glue onto 9. Slide the complete piece into the nose cone.

5 Slip the tailplane (12) into the fuselage. Glue fuselage onto the main wing.

6 Fold up piece 13 and glue it onto the undercarriage to provide enough strength for the plane to stand. Make the hub (14) into a cone and glue onto the wheel.

7 Glue the engine (15) exhausts in place. Cut strips of paper and glue in place to form the cockpit windows.

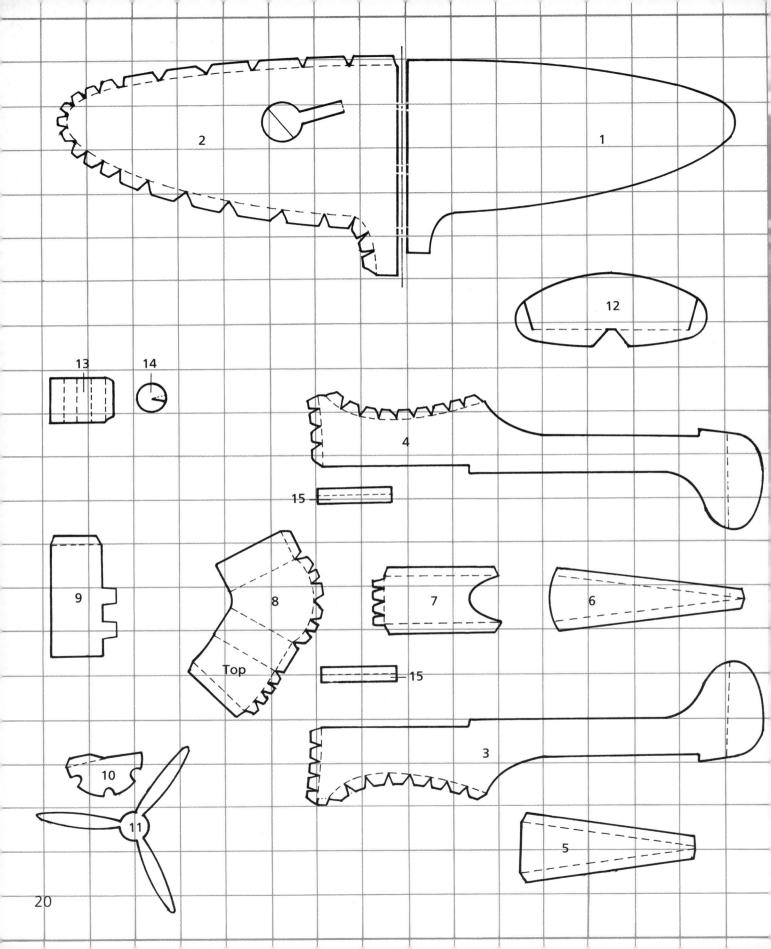

Lockheed
P-38 Lightning

The Lightning has the distinction of being in production throughout the United States involvement in World War II. It had also proved itself to be a remarkable machine before the war began when the prototype completed a United States transcontinental flight in 7 hours 2 minutes flying time on 11 February 1939.

The Lightning was a high performance aircraft. The P-38L, the most numerous sub-type, was powered by two 1,425hp Allison V-1710 engines providing a maximum speed of 414mph, and a climb to 20,000ft in only seven minutes. In addition to all these attributes the P-38L Lightning had great range, some 2,600 miles, enabling it to operate successfully in the Pacific theatre of war against Japan.

Lightning pilots Richard I. Bong and T. B. McGuire became the USAAF's top scoring aces during the conflict. The fighter itself destroyed the most Japanese aircraft of all Allied fighters.

Lockheed
P-38 Lightning

1 Fold and glue the main wing (1).

2 To assemble one engine curve piece 2 before glueing it to pieces 3 and 4.

3 Cut out piece 5 and cut the undercarriage doors. Curve around a dowel then glue to 3 and 4.

4 Cut two of piece 6 and slip in between 3 and 4. Glue in place.

5 Form piece 7 into a ring and glue. Glue the complete piece onto the engine front.

6 Form piece 8 into a ring and glue on to piece 7. Slip piece 9 into piece 8.

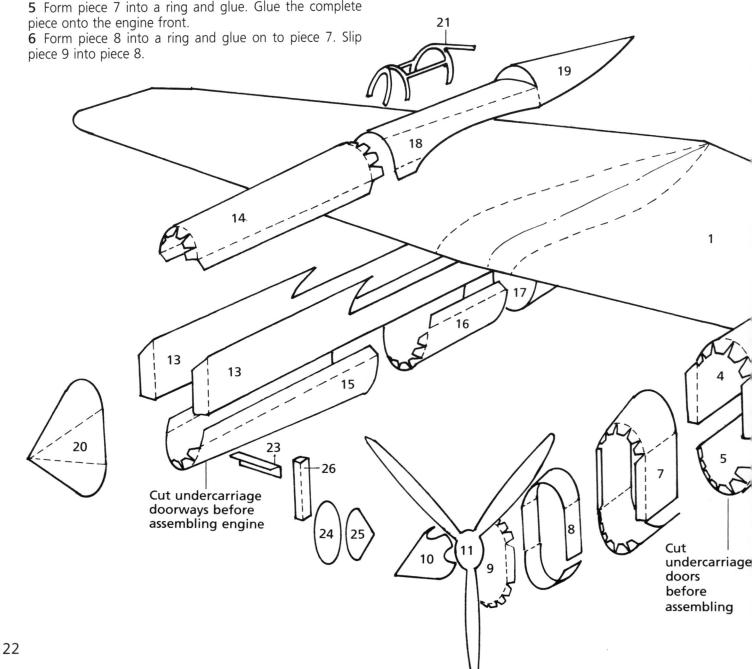

Cut undercarriage doorways before assembling engine

Cut undercarriage doors before assembling

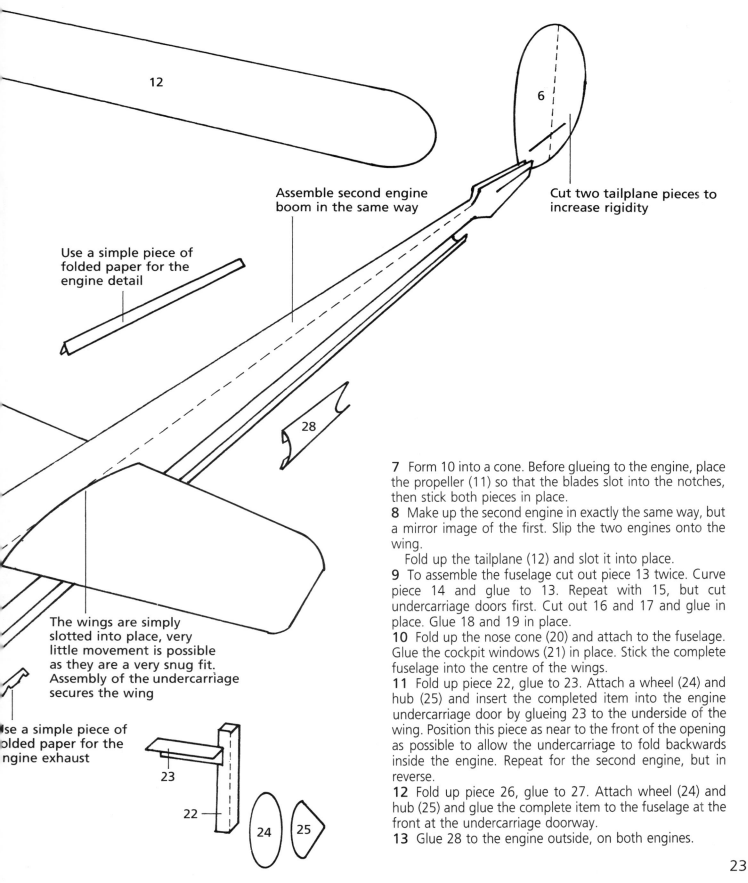

12

6

Assemble second engine boom in the same way

Cut two tailplane pieces to increase rigidity

Use a simple piece of folded paper for the engine detail

28

The wings are simply slotted into place, very little movement is possible as they are a very snug fit. Assembly of the undercarriage secures the wing

Use a simple piece of folded paper for the engine exhaust

23

22

24   25

7 Form 10 into a cone. Before glueing to the engine, place the propeller (11) so that the blades slot into the notches, then stick both pieces in place.

8 Make up the second engine in exactly the same way, but a mirror image of the first. Slip the two engines onto the wing.

Fold up the tailplane (12) and slot it into place.

9 To assemble the fuselage cut out piece 13 twice. Curve piece 14 and glue to 13. Repeat with 15, but cut undercarriage doors first. Cut out 16 and 17 and glue in place. Glue 18 and 19 in place.

10 Fold up the nose cone (20) and attach to the fuselage. Glue the cockpit windows (21) in place. Stick the complete fuselage into the centre of the wings.

11 Fold up piece 22, glue to 23. Attach a wheel (24) and hub (25) and insert the completed item into the engine undercarriage door by glueing 23 to the underside of the wing. Position this piece as near to the front of the opening as possible to allow the undercarriage to fold backwards inside the engine. Repeat for the second engine, but in reverse.

12 Fold up piece 26, glue to 27. Attach wheel (24) and hub (25) and glue the complete item to the fuselage at the front at the undercarriage doorway.

13 Glue 28 to the engine outside, on both engines.

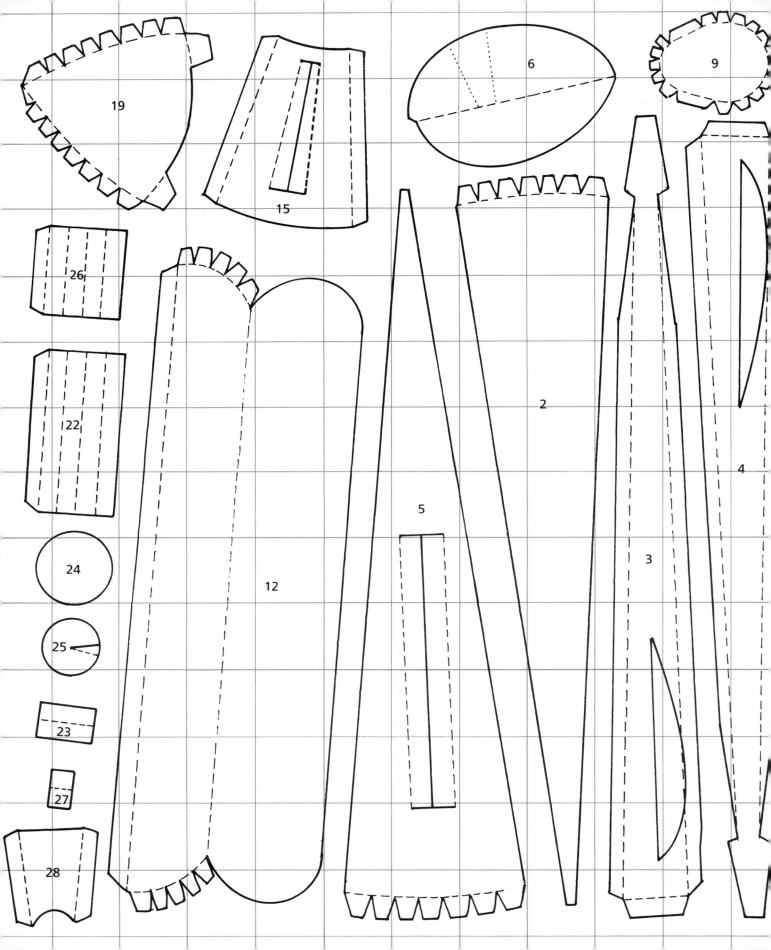

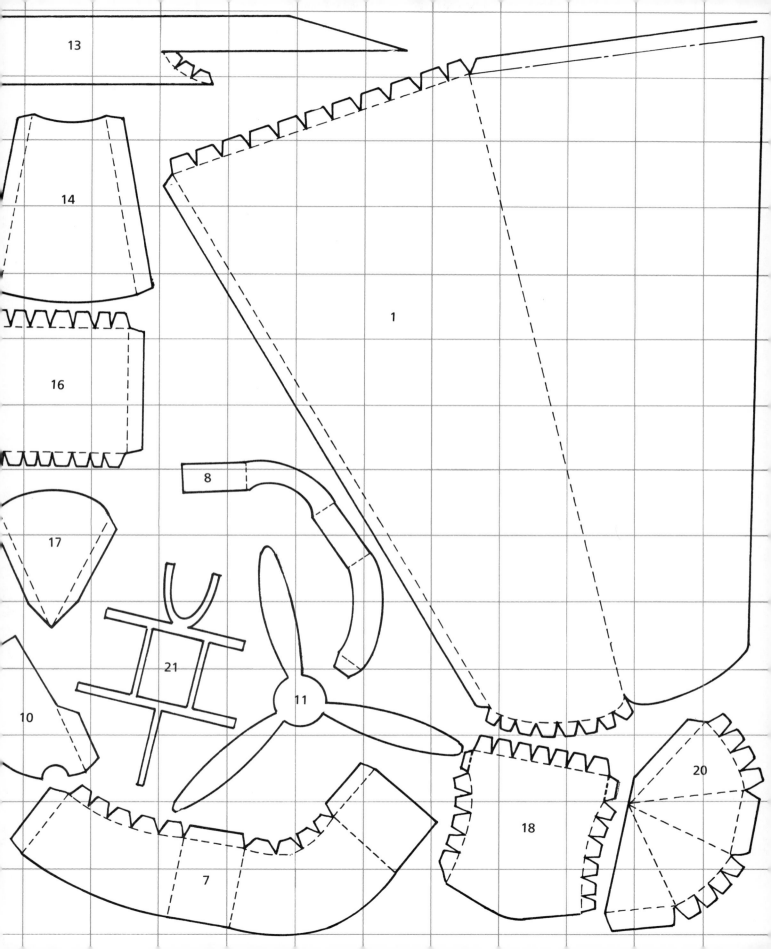

Avro Lancaster

The famous attacks on the Ruhr dams on 17 May 1943, by Lancasters of No 617 Squadron using the 'bouncing bomb' specially designed by Barnes Wallis, is just one episode from the truly illustrious history of the Royal Air Force's most successful heavy bomber.

The Lancaster was a four-engined re-design of the unreliable twin-engined Avro Manchester, which it superseded in service in 1941. The seven-seat heavy bomber was powered by four 1,280hp Rolls-Royce Merlin engines, providing a maximum speed of 275mph, and a range of 2,530 miles with a 7,000lb pay load. The wing span was 102ft and length 69ft 6 inches. Total Lancaster production reached 7,366. The illustration shows the Lancaster that flew more missions than any other, 144, when the average was around twenty.

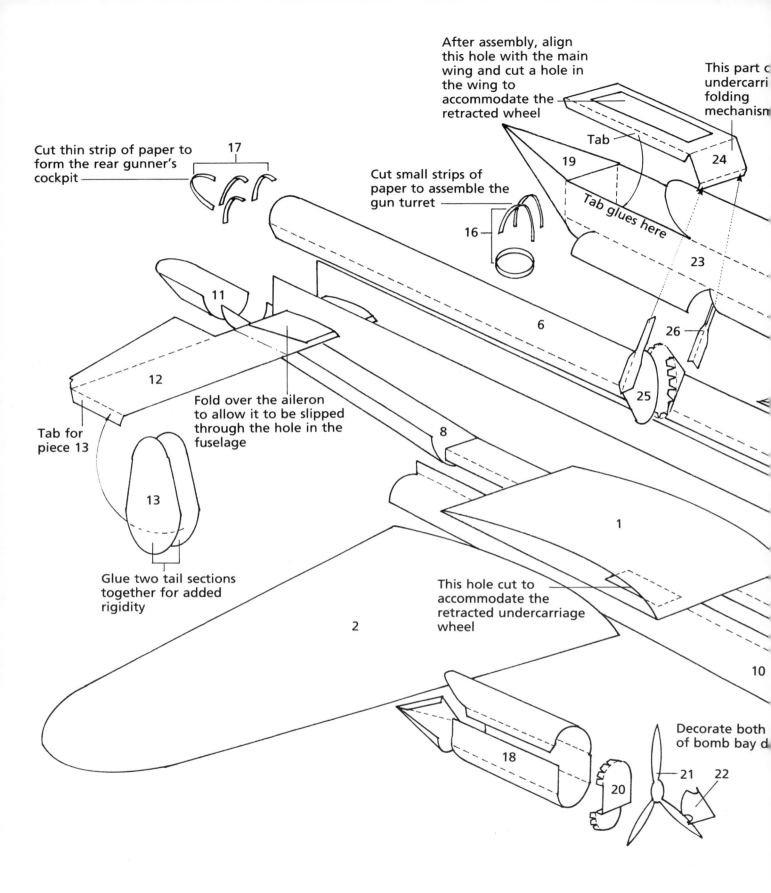

After assembly, align this hole with the main wing and cut a hole in the wing to accommodate the retracted wheel

This part of undercarri folding mechanism

Tab

19

Tab

24

Cut thin strip of paper to form the rear gunner's cockpit

17

Cut small strips of paper to assemble the gun turret

16

Tab glues here

23

11

6

26

12

25

Tab for piece 13

Fold over the aileron to allow it to be slipped through the hole in the fuselage

8

13

1

Glue two tail sections together for added rigidity

This hole cut to accommodate the retracted undercarriage wheel

2

10

18

Decorate both of bomb bay d

20

21   22

Avro Lancaster

1 Cut out main wing centre piece (1). Gently curve the upper part and glue flap to upper.

2 Cut and assemble two each of pieces 2 and 3, gently curving piece 2. Join each complete section to piece 1.

3 Cut out piece 4 twice. Curve piece 5 and glue in place at the front of the fuselage. After curving, glue piece 6 into position. Curve pieces 7 and 8. Glue in place at the front and rear of fuselage. Insert piece 9 into the fuselage between pieces 7 and 8.

4 Piece 10 is the bomb bay door. If you want it to open, curve the two doors *before* cutting in half, cut and glue in position. If you wish the doors to remain closed simply glue into the fuselage in one piece.

5 Fold piece 11 up and glue into place.

6 Assemble tailplane (12). Slot into place in the fuselage. Slot the main wing in place. Complete the tailplane by glueing two of piece 13 in place.

7 Cut out the cockpit windows (14) and glue in place. Using thin strips of paper assemble and attach the front turret, centre turret and rear turret.

Assemble the undercarriage before glueing the engine onto the wing

Take care not to damage the cockpit windows when cutting

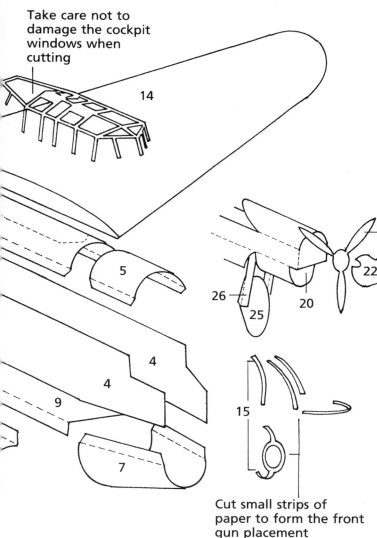

Cut small strips of paper to form the front gun placement

8 The two outer engines (outermost on the wings) are identical, so cut two each of pieces 18–22. To make each engine fold up piece 18, then fold 19 and insert into 18. Glue 20 into 18. Make spinner (22) into a cone, insert propeller (21) into slots and glue these into position.

9 The two engines that contain undercarriages are identical and are assembled in a similar way to the outer engines. Cut out 23. Fold up as for 18, but first cut open the undercarriage doors. Insert pieces 19, 20, 21 and 22 as with the outer engine. Glue piece 24 into the engine. Cut out piece 25 twice, one with tabs, one without and make a wheel. Sandwich it between two pieces 26. Glue this into the engine onto 24. Repeat for the second engine.

10 Glue all the engines in position underneath the wings. When glueing the engines with undercarriage onto the wings, cut a hole into the wing underside to correspond with the hole in piece 24 to accommodate the wheel.

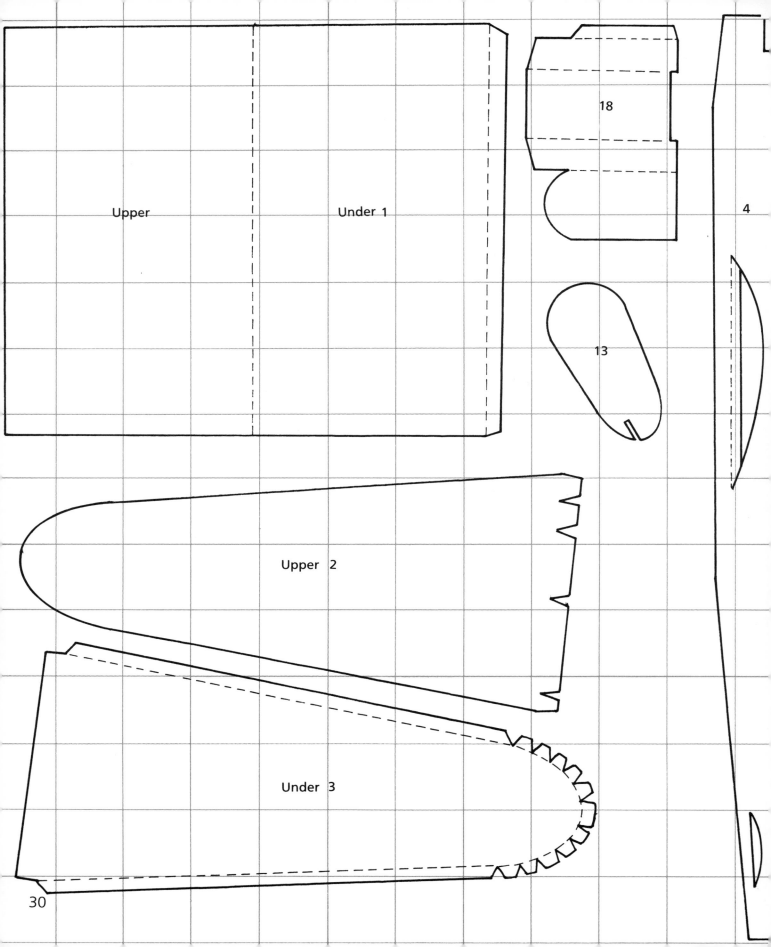

Upper

Under 1

18

4

13

Upper 2

Under 3

30

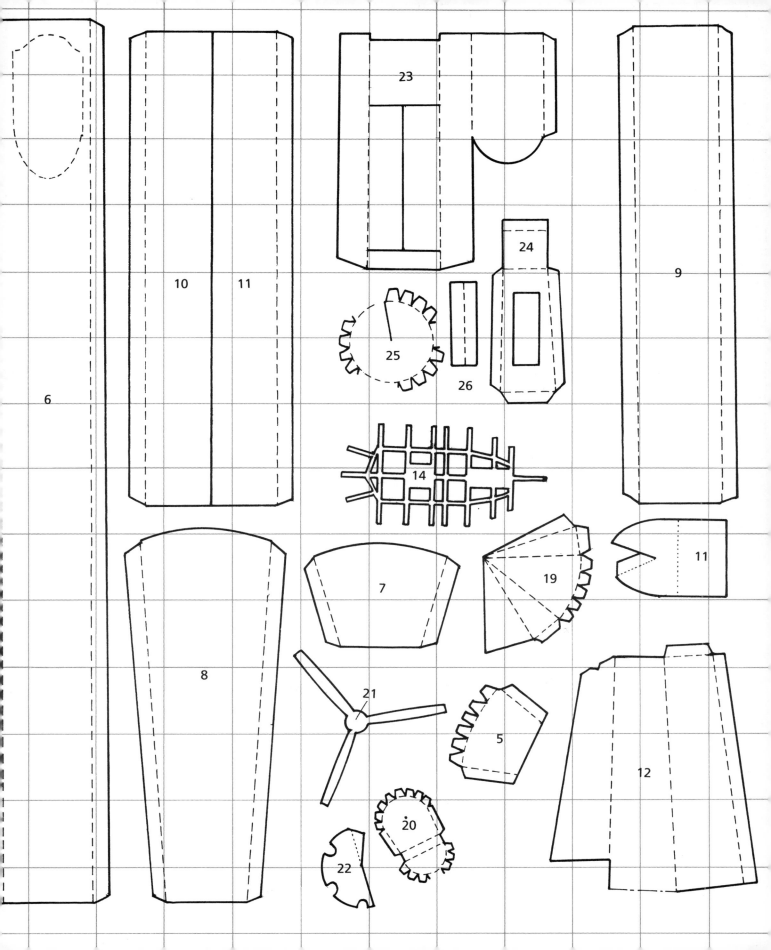

British Aerospace Harrier

Nicknamed the 'Jump Jet' because of its remarkable and revolutionary vertical take-off ability, the Harrier is considered to represent as big a breakthrough in warplane development as the jet engine. The properties of vertical take-off allow fundamental changes in tactics employed by air arms. It vastly reduces reliance upon airfields, which are immediate targets in any future conflict. Even fully armed, the Harrier requires only 425ft of runway which can be found in the form of any roadway or open space. The same properties qualify the Harrier as an ideal aircraft to use aboard aircraft carriers. These innovations have been recognised by air forces throughout the world who have bought Harriers in sufficient numbers to make it Britain's most successful post-war aircraft.

A powerful Rolls-Royce Pegasus vectored-thrust engine provides the Harrier with a top speed of 737mph, a range of 3,455 miles (with one flight refuelling) and a ceiling of 50,000ft. The Harrier has a wing span of 25ft 3 inches.

Fokker
Dr 1

Fokker Dr1
and Sopwith Camel

Messerschmitt
Bf 109

Lockheed
P-38 Lightning

Lockheed
C-130 Hercules

Mikoyan Gurevich MiG-21

Messerschmitt Bf 109
and Spitfire

British Aerospace
Harrier

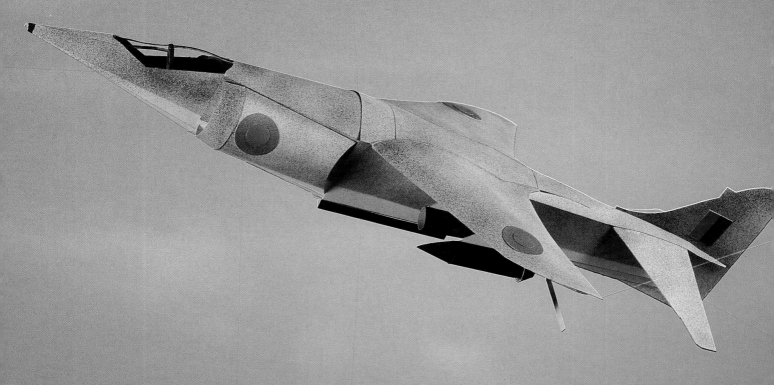

McDonnell Douglas F-15 Eagle

Avro
Lancaster

Bell
UH-1 Huey

General Dynamics
F-111

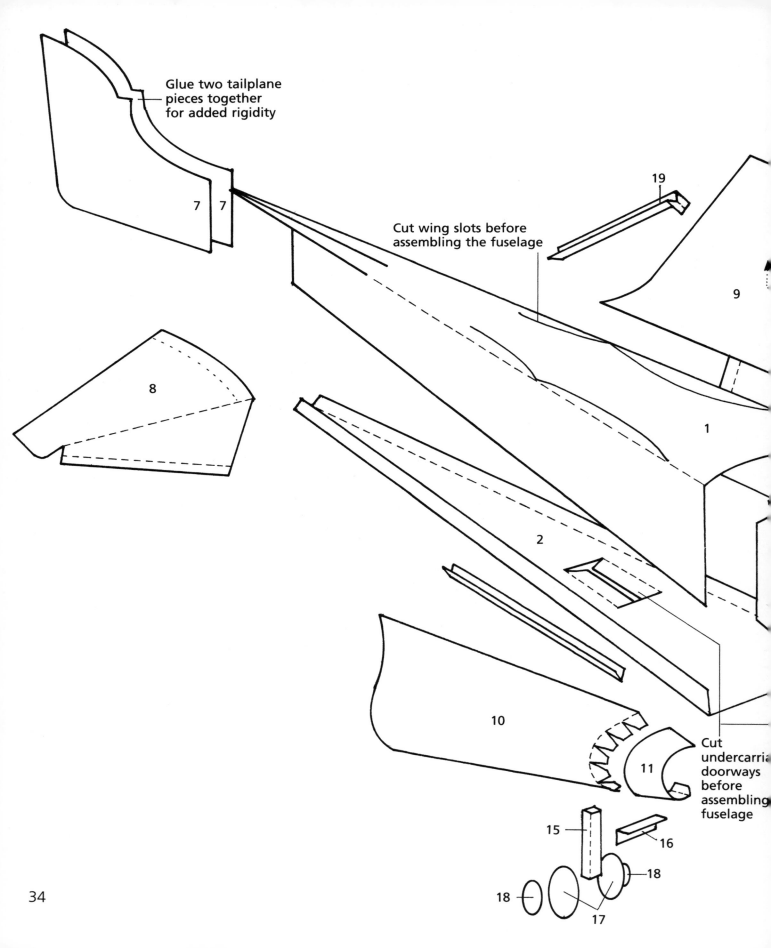

Glue two tailplane
pieces together
for added rigidity

7 | 7

19

Cut wing slots before
assembling the fuselage

9

8

1

2

10

11

Cut
undercarria
doorways
before
assembling
fuselage

15

16

18

18

17

British Aerospace Harrier

1 Fold up piece 1. Cut and fold the undercarriage door in piece 2 before glueing into 1.

2 Cut and fold piece 3. Cut and fold the undercarriage doors in piece 4 before glueing into piece 3.

3 Fold up piece 5 and glue onto fuselage. Glue the cockpit windows (6) in place.

4 Cut out 7 twice. Glue them together and slip into place in the fuselage (1).

5 Fold up the tailplane (8) and glue in place. Repeat this with a mirror image piece for the other side.

6 Fold up the main wing (9). Glue it into place in the slots in the fuselage (1). Repeat with a mirror image piece for the second wing.

7 Join pieces 10 and 11 together to form the engine. Attach the complete piece to piece 3. Once again repeat with mirror image pieces for the second engine.

8 To make the front undercarriage fold up piece 12, glue it to 14 and slot the wheel (13) in place. Glue the finished piece into the doorway in piece 4 at the front of the opening.

9 The rear undercarriage is assembled in the same way from pieces 15, 16 and two each of 17 and 18. Glue piece 19 to each wing tip.

10 Assemble the armaments (20, 21, 22 and 23) and attach them to the wing undersides.

Assemble aircraft armaments and position them after wing is glued into position

23

23

22

20

20

21

3

6

5

4

14

12

13

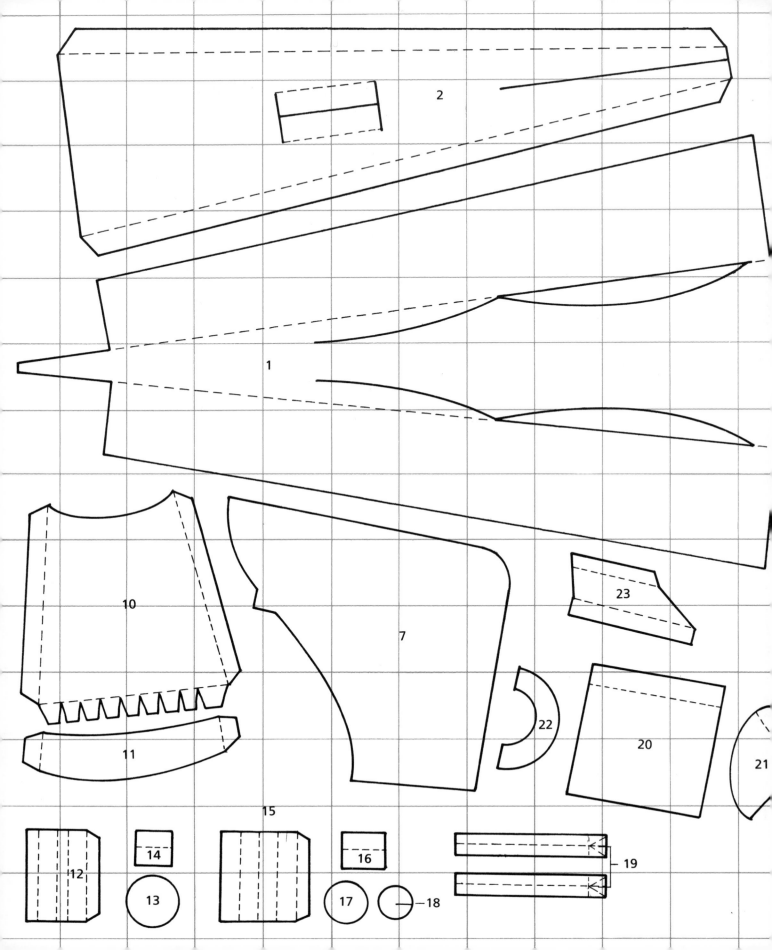

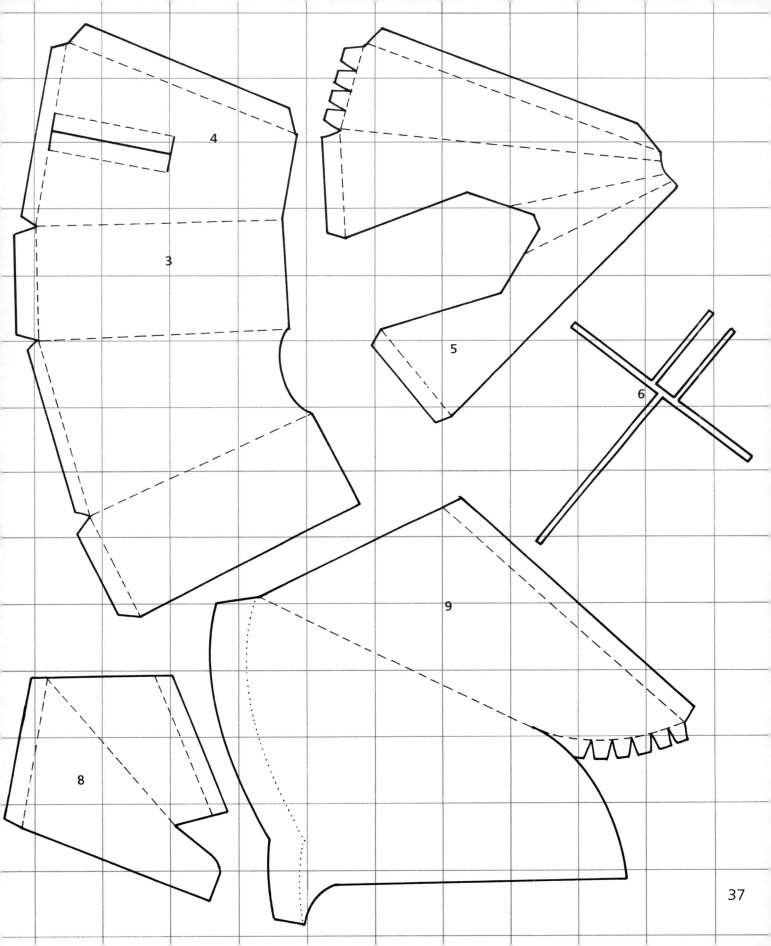

37

Bell
UH-1 Huey

Helicopters were first used for military purposes during the Korean War, but it was not until the American intervention in Vietnam that their potential was fully realised.

First introduced into service in 1962, the 'Huey' was adapted for a variety of jobs – over two thousand flew in Vietnam. They were used as transportation vehicles both for men and *materiel.* Heavily armed, they were used to support troops in the field. These helicopters often provided the only support line for isolated outposts, delivering everything from ammunition to beer.

'Medevac' Hueys flew into the toughest of positions to evacuate wounded and rush them to hospital. Showing scant respect for the Red Cross symbol, these helicopters often dropped ammunition before picking up wounded – 'preventive medicine'. This disrespect for the Red Cross was not confined to the US – the Viet Cong used the crosses as targets. However, once in the field the 'Medevac' teams would evacuate wounded regardless of their nationality or political beliefs.

In 1969, a Huey set the helicopter speed record of 316mph. At least twelve thousand of these durable machines were built, more than any other helicopter model – and more than any fixed wing military aircraft since World War II.

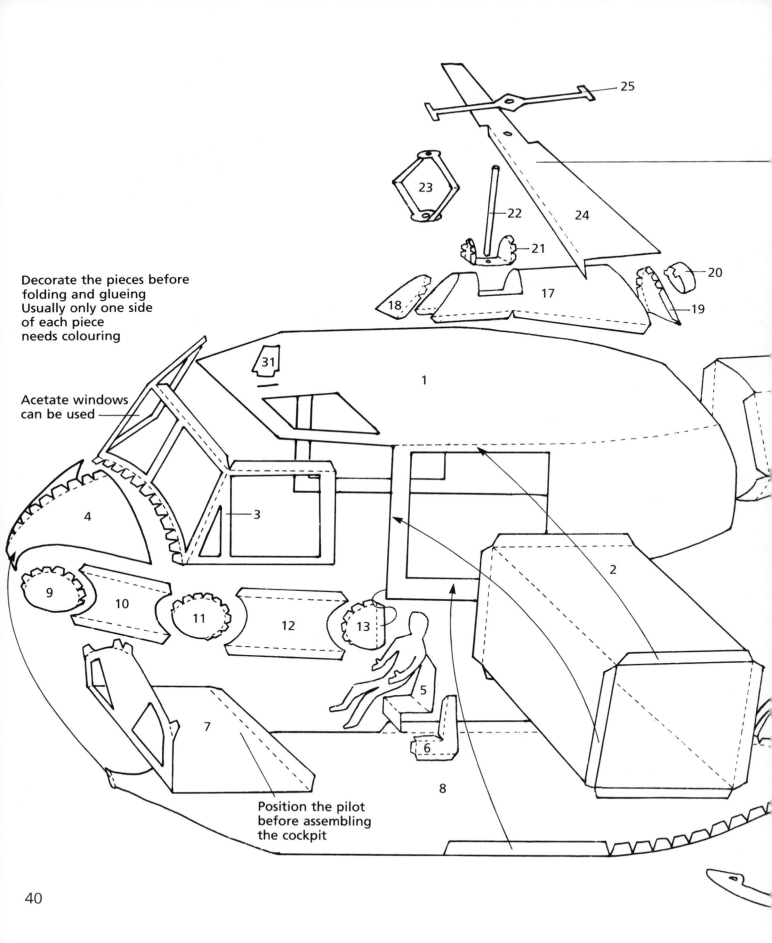

Decorate the pieces before
folding and glueing
Usually only one side
of each piece
needs colouring

Acetate windows
can be used

Position the pilot
before assembling
the cockpit

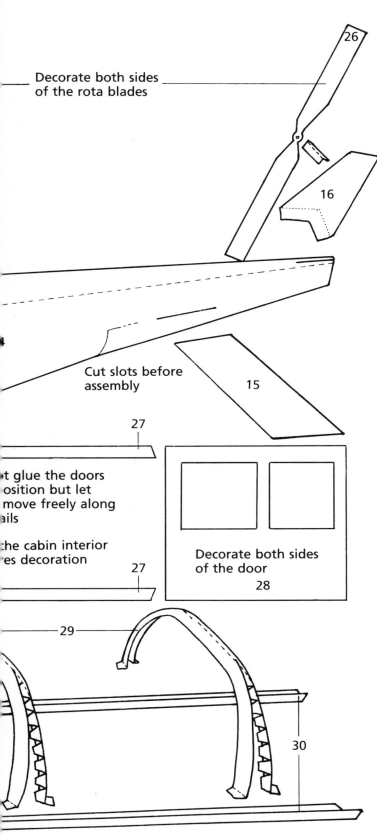

Decorate both sides
of the rota blades

26

16

Cut slots before
assembly

15

27

t glue the doors
osition but let
move freely along
ails

he cabin interior
es decoration

27

Decorate both sides
of the door

28

29

30

Bell UH-1 Huey

1 Fold the body (1). Fold the cabin interior (2) and glue in place within the body.

2 Glue the windows (3) into place. Glue 4 onto the windows.

3 Assemble the pilot's seat 5, 6, and glue in place on the cockpit interior 7. Glue the pilot in place.

4 Insert the cockpit interior behind the window glueing it onto 4 and 2.

5 Glue the helicopter base (8) in position.

6 Assemble the front fuselage by positioning pieces 9, 10, 11, 12, and 13. Repeat for the opposite side, using mirror image pieces.

7 Assemble the tail (14). Slot 15 in place and slip the tail-plane (16) into position.

8 Make up the engine by curving 17 and inserting 18 at the front and 19 at the rear. Make a ring of piece 20 and glue in place on 19. Insert 21. Glue the complete assembly onto the fuselage.

9 Make a tight roll of paper (22). Cut a tiny incision into the engine and fuselage. Thread 23, the rotor blade 24 and counterbalance weight 25 onto the spindle (22). Slot the spindle in place in the engine.

10 Attach the rear rotor blade 26.

11 Cut the skis from a heavier paper (or double thickness) for support. Assemble them as illustrated and glue on to the base of the helicopter.

12 Glue the door rails (27) in place above and below the cabin entrance. Slide the door (28) into the rails.

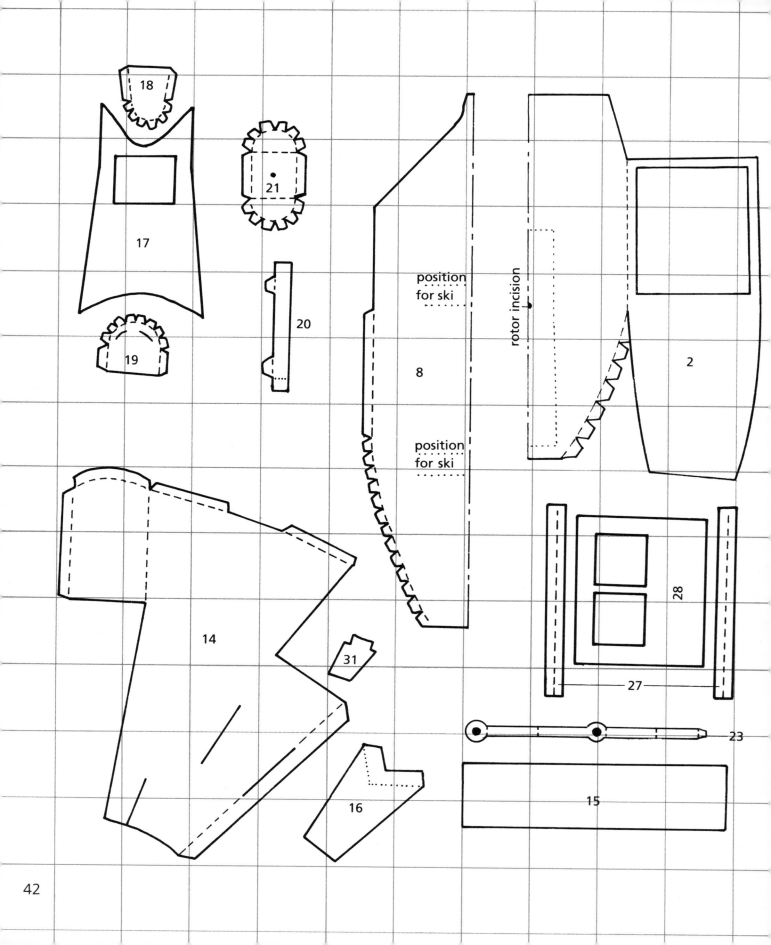

18

17

21

19

20

position
for ski

rotor incision

position
for ski

8

2

14

31

28

27

16

23

15

42

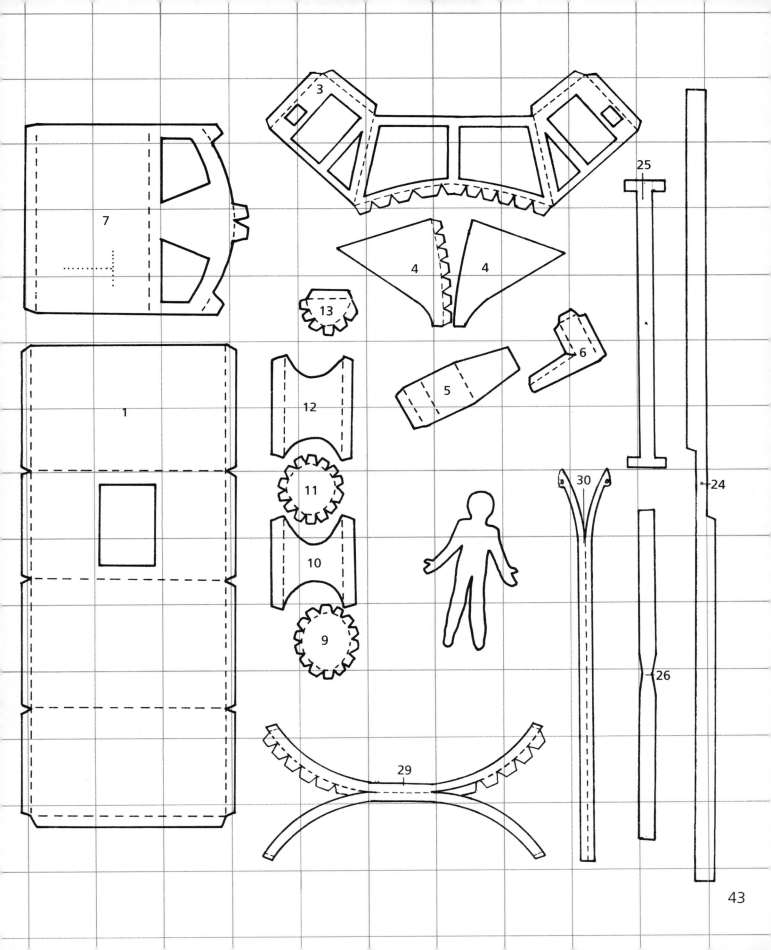

43

Lockheed
C-130 Hercules

Although, perhaps the most familiar image of the Hercules is with dozens of paratroopers falling from the back doorway at air displays, this powerful transport has seen many uses since its introduction to the United States Air Force in 1954. It has carried men and equipment, supplies, armaments, famine relief and a huge diversity of cargo for war and peace. Hercules have been fitted with high definition camera equipment for night surveillance and later with radar scanners.

A heavily-armed gunship version flew in Vietnam. This model was filled with highly complex equipment – image intensifiers, moving target indicators and advanced fire computers. Given the power of the Hercules, the armament was truly daunting, varying from 20mm cannon to 105mm Howitzers, with laser target finders. The aircraft is powered by four 4,500hp engines giving a maximum speed of 380mph and a range of 2,290 miles. The wing span is 132ft 7 inches.

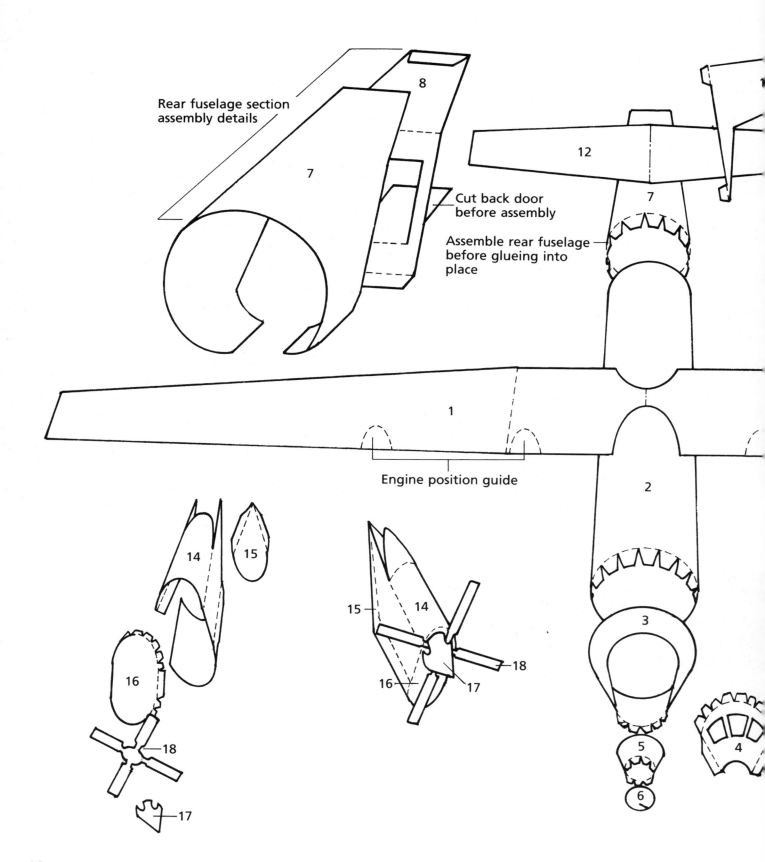

Rear fuselage section
assembly details

8

7

Cut back door
before assembly

Assemble rear fuselage
before glueing into
place

12

7

1

Engine position guide

2

14

15

15

14

18

16

17

16

18

17

3

5

4

6

Glue two tail sections
together for added rigidity

Lockheed
C-130 Hercules

1 Cut out, fold up and glue the main wing (1). (This can be done as one piece or three, whichever you find easiest. If done in three remember to leave a tab to join the pieces – shown as a dotted line on the plan.)

2 Roll fuselage (2) into a cylinder. Cut the wing slot and fold the undercarriage doors before gluing.

3 Form piece 3 into a ring and glue onto fuselage. Insert piece 4 into 3. Form piece 5 into a ring, glue onto 3. Make piece 6 into a cone, glue onto 5.

4 Roll the fuselage rear section (7) into a ring. Insert the doorway (8) and glue the completed section onto 2.

5 Cut out 9. Cut out two of piece 10 and glue them into each end of 9. Glue a piece 11 onto each undercarriage doorway. Glue the completed section onto the underside of the fuselage.

6 Slip the main wing (1) into place on the fuselage (2).

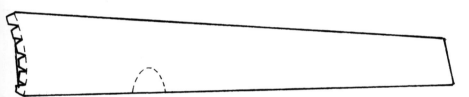

11   10

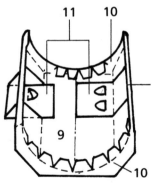

Assemble undercarriage
section before glueing
to the underside of the
fuselage

9

10

20
19
21

7 Fold up the tailplane (12) and glue onto 7. Cut out two of 13, glue together and position.

As all the engines are identical, only one is included in the plan. Each piece is cut four times, one for each engine. Naturally they are all assembled in the same way.

8 Cut out 14, fold into shape and glue. Glue pieces 15 and 16 into position. Fold piece 17 into a cone. Glue onto the engine sandwiching the propeller (18) in place as you do so. Position each complete engine on the main wing.

9 To assemble the front undercarriage cut out and fold piece 19 and glue onto 20. Attach two wheels (21). Glue the complete piece to the front of the undercarriage doorway.

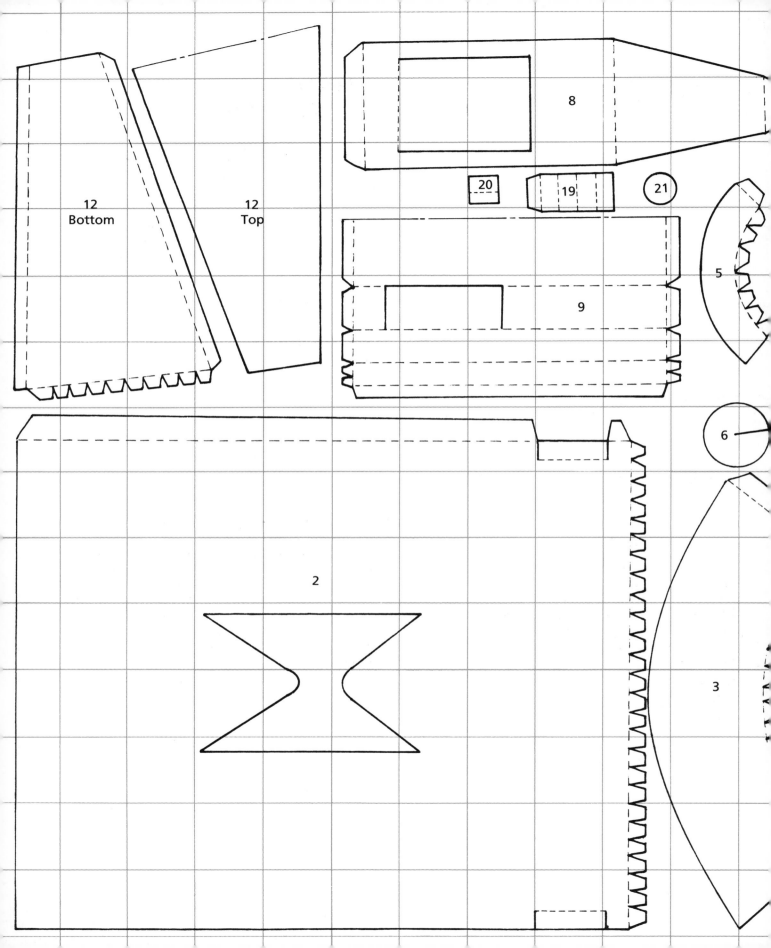

12
Bottom

12
Top

8

20

19

21

9

5

6

2

3

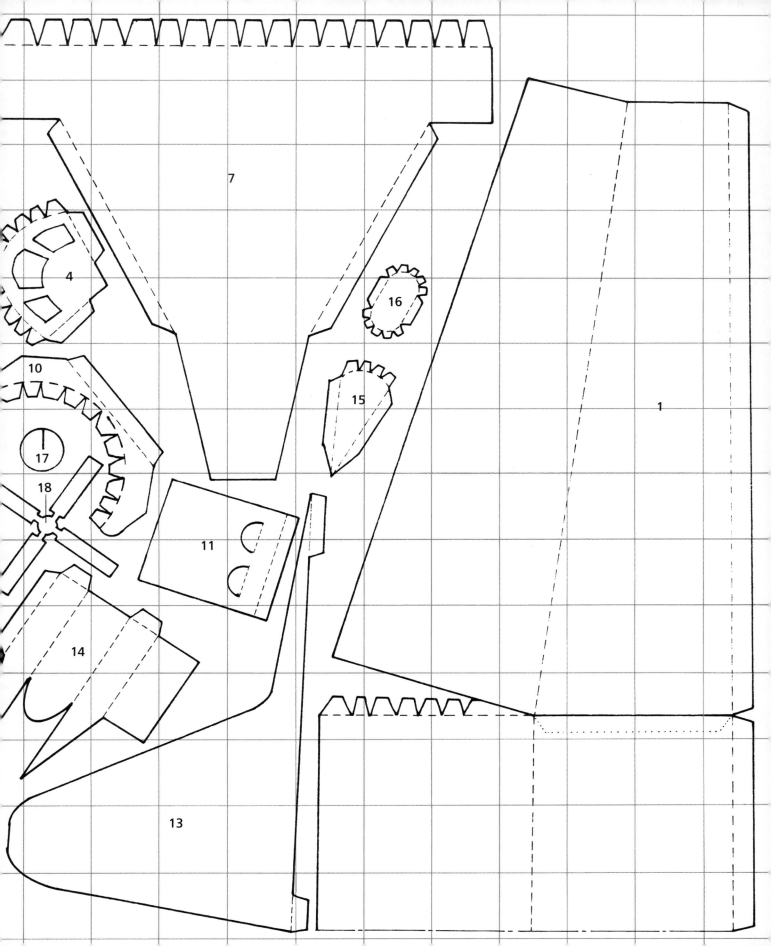

Mikoyan Gurevich MiG-21

Over 10,000 MiG-21s have been built since their inception in 1957, making it the most numerous fighter in the world today. The MiG-21 has been operated in combat situations by India, North Vietnam, Egypt and Syria, but this represents only a fraction of the nations around the world who either have deployed or presently still deploy the aircraft. The Soviet Union still operates a great number of the aircraft, despite having made considerable advances in warplane technology.

During the peak years of its deployment, the power supplied by a 16,535lb-thrust Tumanskii engine providing a maximum speed of 1,385mph, good manoeuvrability coupled with a range of 720 miles, the MiG-21 made a significant tactical aircraft. However, the arrival of modern US fighters, such as the F-14 Tomcat and F-15 Eagle and major technological advances in Soviet aircraft have lessened the MiG-21's strategic importance.

Mikoyan Gurevich MiG-21

1 Cut out and assemble the main wing from pieces 1 and 2.

2 Cut out the fuselage (3) and form into a cylinder, first cutting the wing slot and undercarriage slots.

3 Cut out the engine (4), cut the tailplane slots, then fold into shape and glue onto fuselage.

4 Fold the nose cone (5) into shape and glue. Cut out the air intake (6 and 7). Insert piece 6 into the wide end of piece 5, push in as far as it will go and glue. Fold 7 into a cone and slip it into the front of piece 5 glueing it onto piece 6.

5 Gently curve pieces 8 and 9 and glue onto fuselage. Glue piece 10 onto the engine.

6 Cut two of piece 11, glue them together and then glue onto piece 10. In the same way cut piece 12 out twice, glue these together and then onto piece 4.

7 Fold up the tailplane (13) and slot into place in piece 4.

8 Cut out the cockpit (14) and glue onto piece 3.

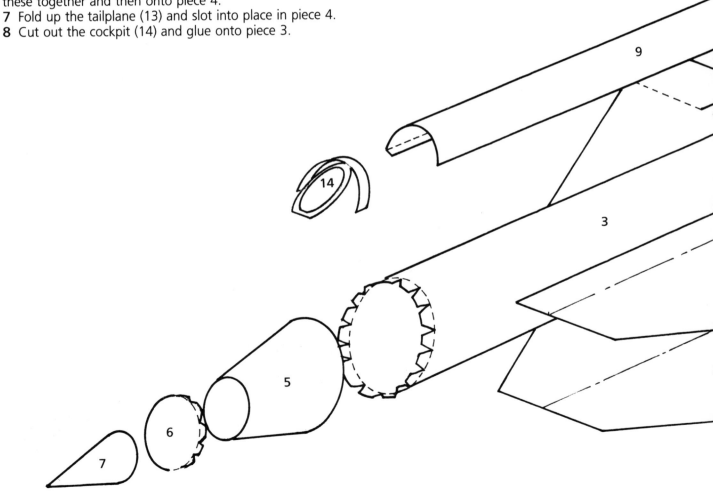

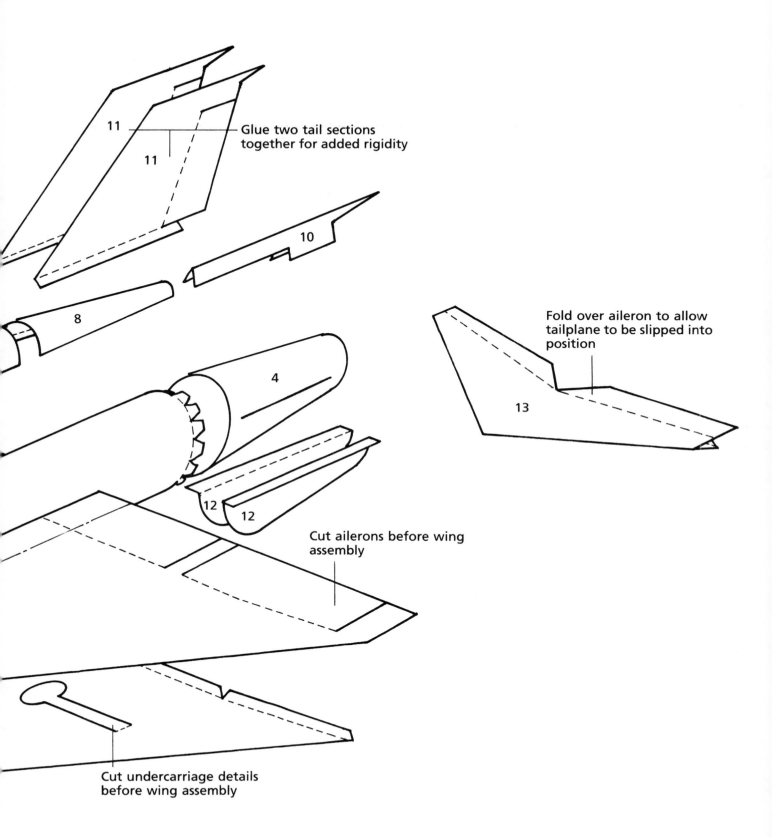

11

Glue two tail sections
together for added rigidity

11

10

8

4

Fold over aileron to allow
tailplane to be slipped into
position

13

12

12

Cut ailerons before wing
assembly

Cut undercarriage details
before wing assembly

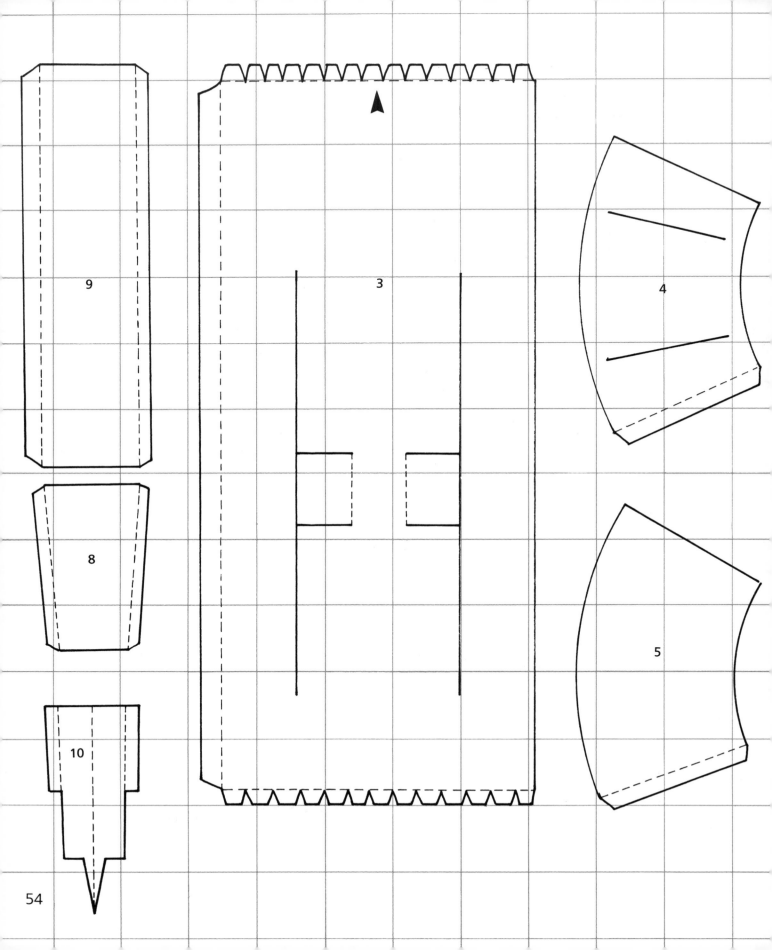

9

3

4

8

5

10

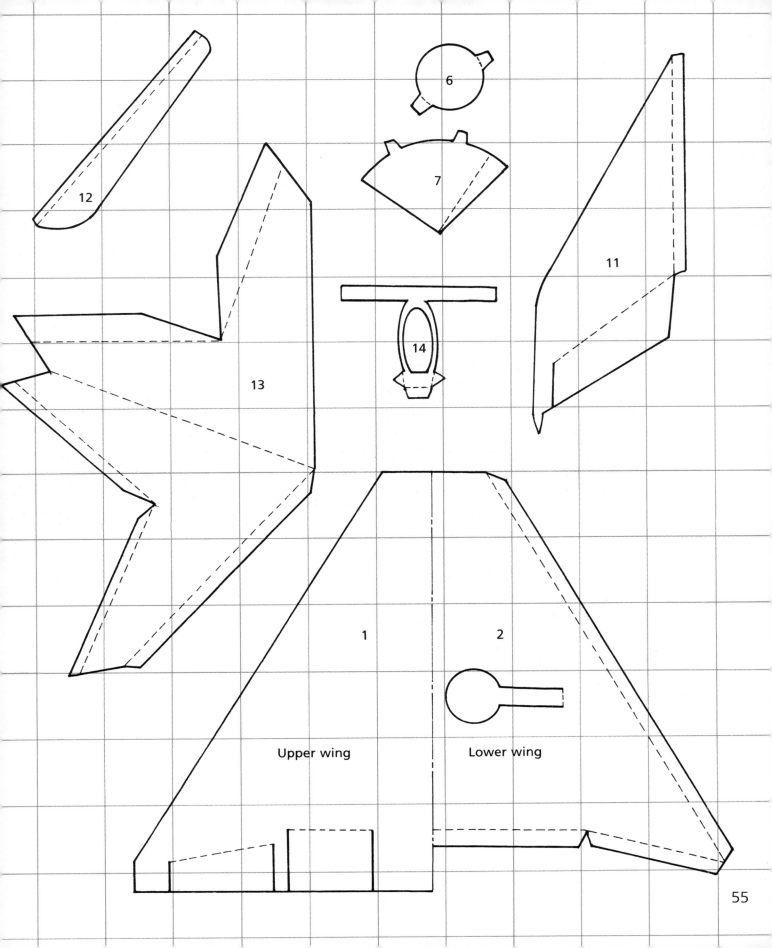

6

7

12

11

13

14

1

2

Upper wing

Lower wing

55

McDonnell Douglas F-15 Eagle

The Eagle has been designed to gain total superiority through air-to-air combat and in this role is only rivalled by another American aircraft, the F-14 Tomcat. Operated by the United States Air Force throughout the world, the Eagle has seen service in the air forces of other nations such as Saudi Arabia, Japan and Israel, the latter using the fighter in action over the Lebanon. To date, the Eagle has scored many victories for no loss, this success being due to the aircraft's remarkable performance, provided by two 25,000lb-thrust engines and advanced aerodynamics. A maximum speed of 1,650mph, high manoeuvrability and an advanced and comprehensive armament combine to create a truly formidable 'state of the art' fighter aircraft.

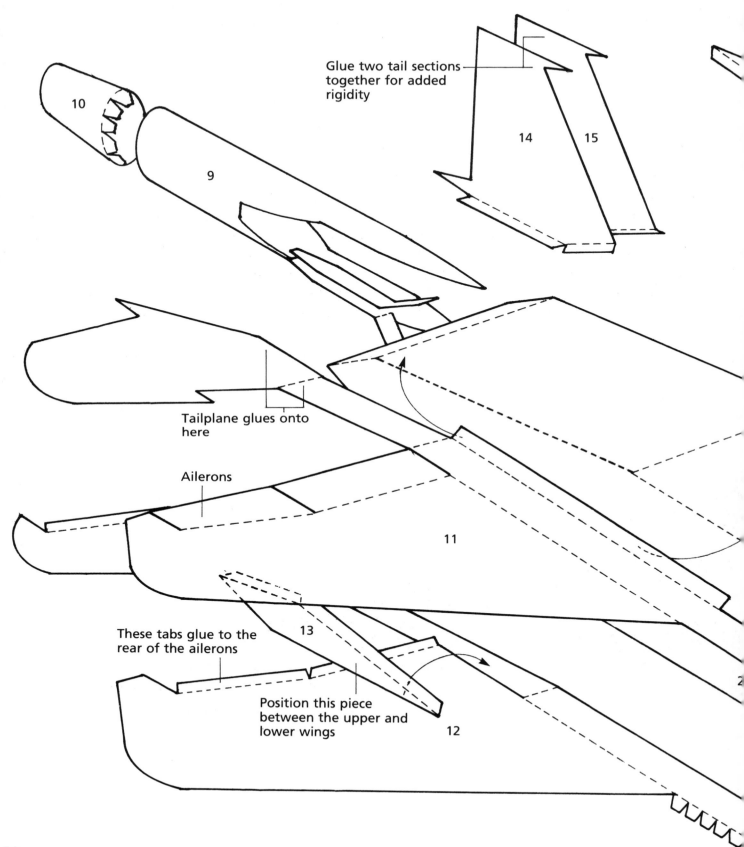

Glue two tail sections together for added rigidity

10

9

14   15

Tailplane glues onto here

Ailerons

11

These tabs glue to the rear of the ailerons

13

Position this piece between the upper and lower wings

12

McDonnell Douglas F-15 Eagle

1 Cut out fuselage (1). Fold in the sides and glue the underside (2) in place.

2 Cut out pieces 3 and 4 and glue into place.

3 Form piece 5 into a cylinder. Make a cone from 6 and glue it to piece 5. Join the complete piece to the front of the fuselage (1).

4 Glue cockpit pieces 7 and 8 in place on piece 5.

5 Both the engines are identical so you will need to cut two each of pieces 9 and 10. Form piece 9 into a cylinder and piece 10 into a ring. Join the two pieces and slip the complete engine onto the back of the fuselage (1).

6 Form one wing by joining the upper (11) and underside (12) together, sandwiching piece 13 in place. Join the complete wing assembly to the fuselage. Repeat for the second wing, but join the parts to make it a mirror image of the first.

7 Stick pieces 14 and 15 together and glue onto the tailplane. Repeat this for the second tailplane.

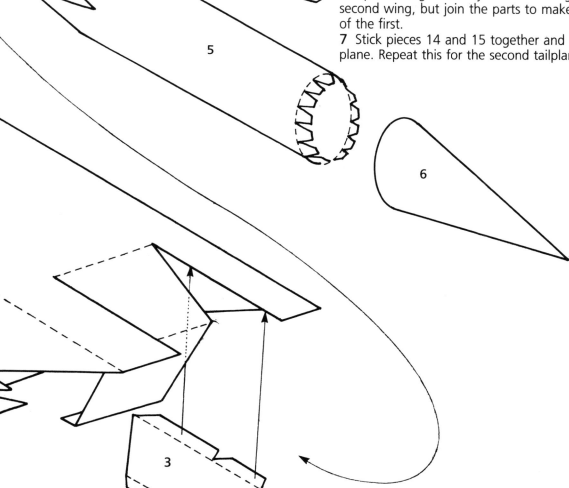

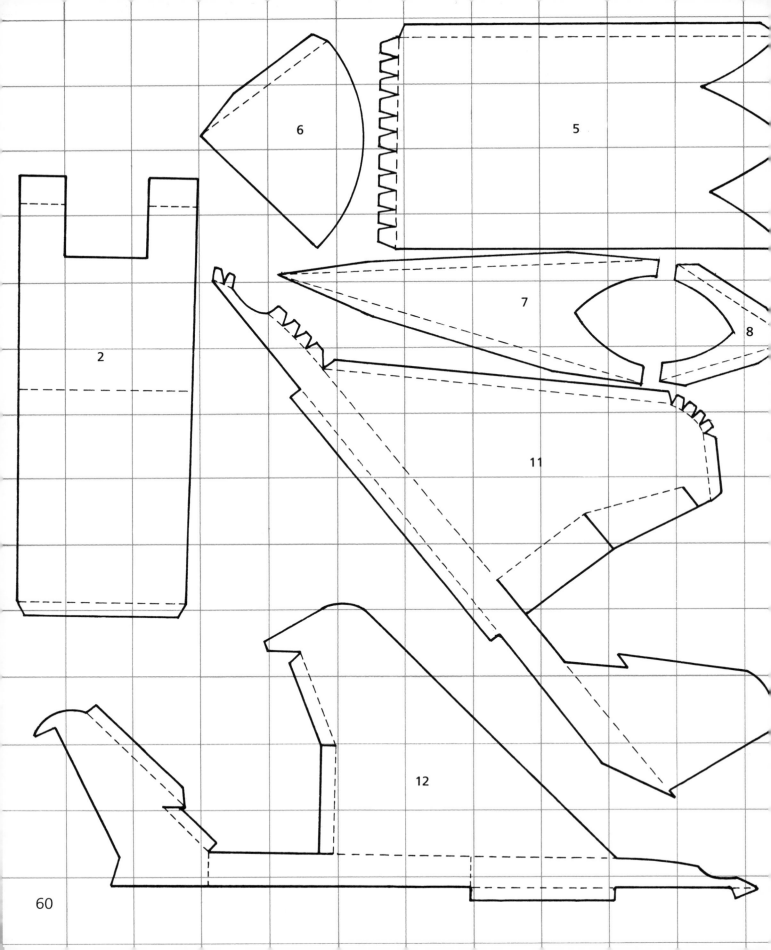

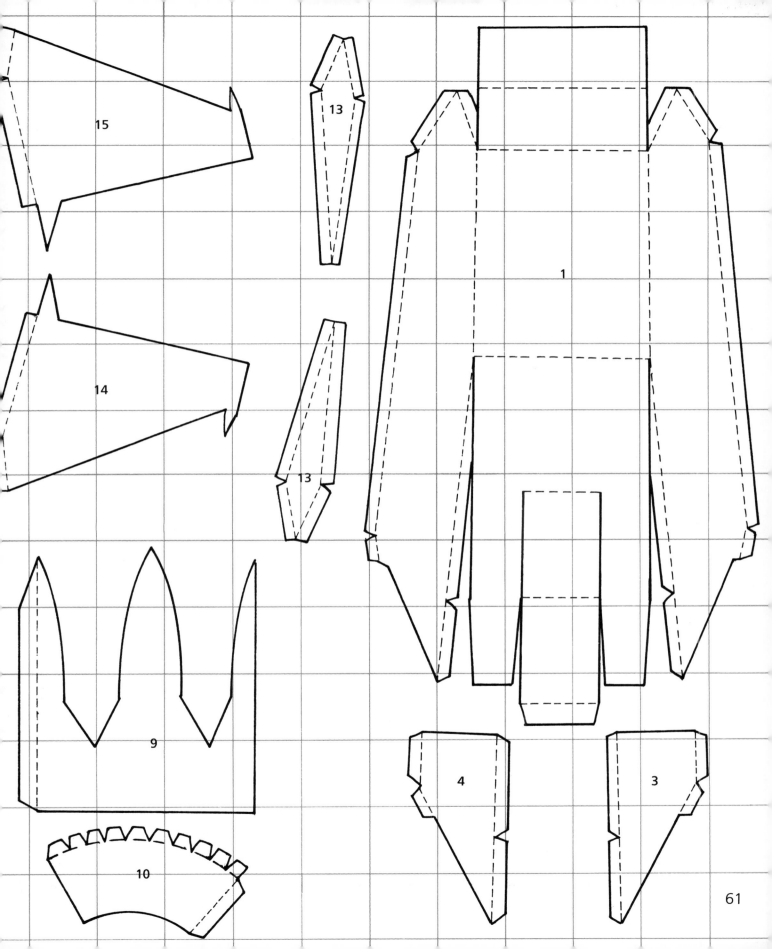

15

13

1

14

13

9

4

3

10

61

General Dynamics F-111

The F-111 demonstrates how successfully a variable geometry wing can allow great diversity in performance. The wing span can be altered from 63ft spread to only 32ft fully swept.

The initial model, the F-111A, was deployed to Vietnam in 1968 but, as losses were greater than anticipated, the fighter was withdrawn for modifications. After this work was completed, a second squadron was deployed and losses amounted to only six in four thousand missions.

US Air Force F-111s are based in several countries. It was the aircraft used in the controversial 'anti-terrorist' raid launched from England by the United States on Libya in April 1986.

A maximum speed of 912mph is provided by two 18,500lb-thrust engines. The aircraft can be given a nuclear capability in the form of one or two 750lb (340kg) B-43 nuclear bombs.

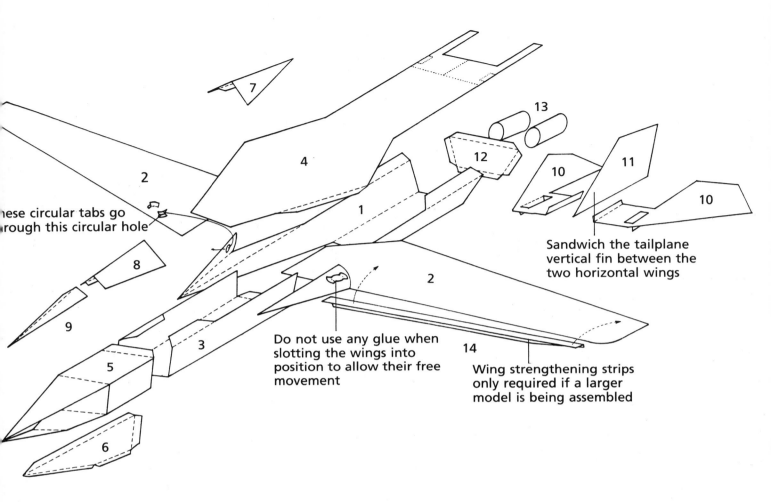

These circular tabs go through this circular hole

Do not use any glue when slotting the wings into position to allow their free movement

Sandwich the tailplane vertical fin between the two horizontal wings

Wing strengthening strips only required if a larger model is being assembled

General Dynamics F-111

1 Cut out the lower fuselage (1). Fold up the wing supports and sandwich the wings (2) in place using the hole and slot device to allow the wings to move forwards and backwards.

2 Glue piece 3 in place under the wings onto the lower fuselage. Glue piece 4 onto 1 and 3.

3 Assemble the nose cone from piece 5 and two of piece 6. Join them to the fuselage.

4 Build the cockpit by glueing piece 7 onto 4 and pieces 8 and 9 onto 5.

5 Cut out piece 10 twice. Glue these onto the body slipping piece 11 in between them to form the tailplane.

6 Glue 12 into position. Cut out piece 13 twice. Form each into a cylinder and glue onto 12 to form the engines.

7 Cut out piece 14 twice. Glue one to the underside of each wing to provide extra strength, ensuring that it does not obstruct the free movement of the wings.

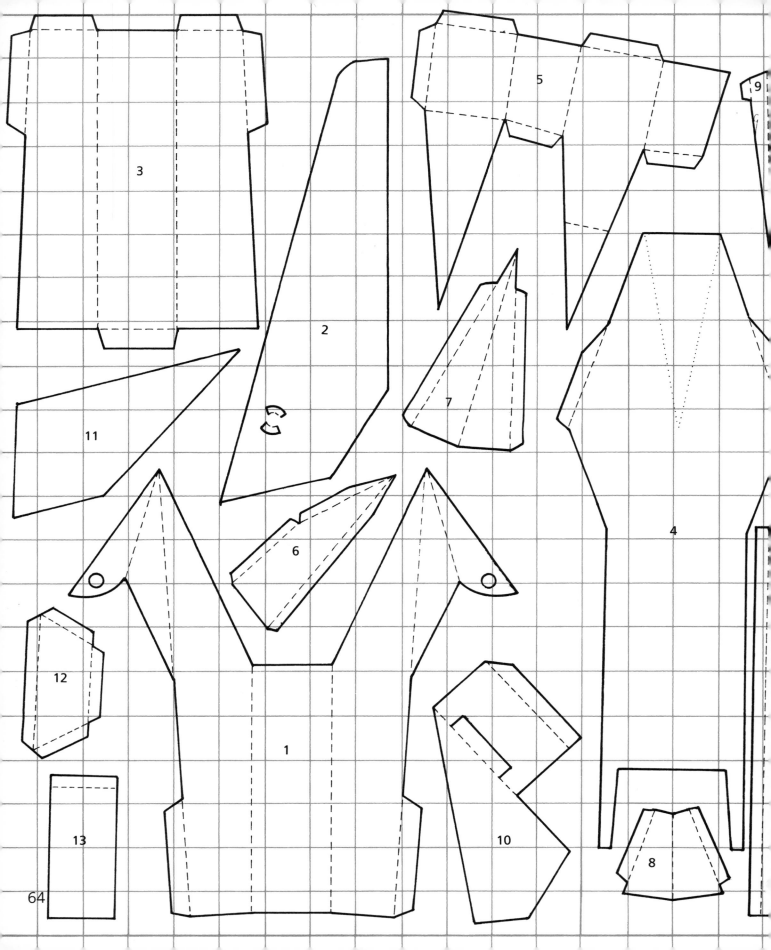

3

5

9

2

11

7

4

6

12

13

1

10

8